THE
MANAGERIAL
LEADERSHIP
JOURNEY

AN **UNCONVENTIONAL**
BUSINESS PURSUIT

JULIAN
CHAPMAN

Advantage.

Published by Advantage, Charleston, South Carolina.
Member of Advantage Media Group.

ADVANTAGE is a registered trademark, and the Advantage colophon is a trademark of Advantage Media Group, Inc.

Printed in the United States of America.

10 9 8 7 6 5 4 3 2 1

ISBN: 978-1-64225-3-313
LCCN: 2022902308

Cover design by Matthew Morse.
Layout design by Analisa Smith.

This publication is designed to provide accurate and authoritative information in regard to the subject matter covered. It is sold with the understanding that the publisher is not engaged in rendering legal, accounting, or other professional services. If legal advice or other expert assistance is required, the services of a competent professional person should be sought.

 Advantage Media Group is proud to be a part of the Tree Neutral® program. Tree Neutral offsets the number of trees consumed in the production and printing of this book by taking proactive steps such as planting trees in direct proportion to the number of trees used to print books. To learn more about Tree Neutral, please visit www.treeneutral.com.

Advantage Media Group is a publisher of business, self-improvement, and professional development books and online learning. We help entrepreneurs, business leaders, and professionals share their Stories, Passion, and Knowledge to help others Learn & Grow. Do you have a manuscript or book idea that you would like us to consider for publishing? Please visit advantagefamily.com.

To Christopher, Amelia, Robert, and Alastair. May you find that great place to work where the managerial leaders are true professionals.

CONTENTS

FOREWORD ix

ACKNOWLEDGMENTS. xiii

INTRODUCTION 1

CHAPTER 1 9
**Managerial Leadership: The Foundation
of an Effective Organization**

CHAPTER 2 29
Managing Managers

CHAPTER 3: 49
**Application of Managerial Accountability:
The Core of Success**

CHAPTER 4 83
**The Engaged Manager: A Manager
of Managers' Day in the Life**

CHAPTER 5 123
The Enlightened Leader: How to Lead People

CHAPTER 6 153
Strategy Operations and Tactics: The Focus of Work

CHAPTER 7 179
Skills of Managerial Leadership

CHAPTER 8 207
The Tools of the Managerial Leader

CONCLUSION 233

FOREWORD

My first exposure to managerial leadership, and by extension to Julian, was in 2015 as a new president. I engaged Julian and Forrest & Company to assist me in building my leadership team.

In the intervening years, he has become a trusted advisor and ongoing executive coach. At first, I was struck by the depth and breadth of his understanding of my business; however, I have come to realize that it is not that he knows *my* business in and out, but that he knows the ways of successful businesses in and out. I find myself continually seeking him out as a sounding board, looking forward to our conversations, debates, and investigations deep into the core of what makes a successful, efficient, effective organization.

Julian's greatest contribution to my thinking about business has been the notion of managerial leadership. This meshes the two complementary but very different practices of management and leadership with the aim of getting the work done properly the first time, providing our people with clarity, and unleashing the potential of the organization.

While the concept of managerial leadership is not new, it has, in recent years, been competing for space with the thinking that management is a tool of the twentieth century and is unimportant in comparison to leadership.

Julian long ago convinced me that leadership is a wonderful thing, but great leadership will likely all be for naught *if the work isn't getting done*. It is the main reason for his belief that management needs to be a profession; just as other disciplines have. Management focuses itself on task, whereas leadership focuses on people. Only with a combination of the two can we hope to be truly successful.

These practices are universal to business and work across any industry. They are tested, proven, and rooted in industrial psychology. They are pragmatic, results-driven, and provide more clarity and less ambiguity to employees. Ultimately, this decreases anxiety and stress, increases employee engagement, and creates a great place to work.

Practicing managerial leadership is, quite simply, a performance accelerator and multiplier.

This book presents the practices and ideas that Julian has shared with me over the years in a concise and actionable form. The work between these pages is not hard to understand but can appear daunting and requires ongoing commitment. It requires changing mindsets, challenging how things have been done before, a firm grasp of who is accountable for what, and the willingness to hold them accountable for that.

Central to this book is the role of the manager's manager. It is here where accountability has become the foundation for our business and its success. As Julian says in chapter 3, *"Accountability distinguishes the professional from the amateur"* and how we lead our leaders defines just how successful we will be.

The core of this book is the foundation of my "playbook" for our business. Through it, we have made a commitment to the path and seen immediate benefits and payoffs. For us, *"the force multiplier of organizational success is aligned management."* The road is long, and the world can get in the way, but Julian has consistently pushed me to carry on and implement my playbook with great effect. I have trusted Julian not only with my own development as a managerial leader, but in the development of many of my senior team leaders as well. Every day, we root ourselves and our actions in the learnings you will find in this book, and cascade it down through our organization right to the managers on the bakery floor. This holistic approach ensures the business runs with a common language, a collective purpose, and a vision and mission that benefit the individual, the team, and the organization equally.

Julian's approach is reflected well in this book. His extensive experience in both the military and with countless businesses has been captured here to the reader's benefit. His ability to speak with, and relate to, people at all levels of the business serves his clients well and reminds you that you are in very capable and experienced hands. Julian is providing you with the tools, and it's to your benefit to pick them up.

I encourage you to read this book with the same intensity and straightforwardness that Julian would bring to you in person. His calls to action are just that, prompts to find the pain points in your organization—be it wasted meetings, lack of decisions, resource squabbles or failing to deliver your strategy—and work to remove that pain from the organization. Only by removing the sources of organizational pain can we create great places to work.

–**Tyson Yu**
Chief Executive Officer, Aspire Bakeries

ACKNOWLEDGMENTS

Writing these acknowledgments was almost harder than the book itself, having to balance brevity while ensuring that I miss no one. It is hard to sum up nearly forty years in this field and to recognize all those who have had a personal impact on you. I learned a long time ago that publicly naming one person is risky because you inevitably forget someone else.

I have girded myself for this, so here we go. I want to thank those who encouraged me to write a book. Most notably, Nick Forrest founded Forrest & Company and told me not to wait as long for my first book as he had. Then there was my coach Paul Tremlett, a recent addition to the Forrest team. When Paul became my coach, he chided me every time we met with the question, "Where is that book?"

From time to time, some clients recommended writing a book because the world would never believe what was happening in their businesses. Rather abashedly, I must admit some clients also thought I had something to say.

My recent coach was Suzanna de Boer in France, who challenged and encouraged me to write the whole book and specifically chapter 6 because she felt it needed to be told. In that vein, I want to thank my editor, Stephen Larkin, and the team at Advantage for taking the shell that Suzanna and I worked on and bringing it into its current form.

I would also like to thank our clients, especially Tyson Yu for his foreword, and those who have given testimonials. I have been careful not to expose any particular client, but working with so many in my twenty years at Forrest & Company has taught me a tremendous amount. The lessons of business leadership come from our clients. The time with them has given me an outstanding education in food production, perfumery, mining, insurance, charities, natural gas, HVAC, banking, retail, aircraft design, and marketing, to name a few.

There are those who I need to acknowledge for the insight they gave me and for what they taught me along the way. Most notable is Jerry Rhodes, the founder of Effective Intelligence, who, at his home in Wotton-under-Edge in Gloucestershire, spent weeks over various years teaching me the nature of thinking and how to be better at it and almost gave me a baccalaureate degree in the classics. To round out this understanding, Herb Koplowitz and Michael Anderson of the Forrest team embedded the managerial leadership notions from Elliott Jaques's *Requisite Organization*.

All those who helped me during my thirty-four-year military career deserve a special thank-you. The names are too many to include here. That said, the most important were those who served under me over the decades. I truly had the honor to lead the finest soldiers in the world. They never let me down, regardless of how difficult the tasks. All those direct reports and the thousands under my command have taught me the real management and leadership lessons. While I made mistakes along the way, it was often at their expense. I thank them, though, because they still came out the next day for another go with the same enthusiasm they had before things went wrong.

The Forrest team needs a special mention. This book would not have happened without them. My business partner, Tony Welsh, honed the content over the years. He always has a designer eye on expressing the most complex constructs and pushed me to write at a certain cost to the business. Jason Legere has been by my side for a lot of the content and was instrumental in preparing to launch this book. Our chief of staff Marsali Federico has been a great writing partner, and I truly valued her view of the book. The stalwart Katherine Pearce and Salman Haider ran our back offices and ensured that I had materials and was prepared for client sessions while my mind was still locked in chapters. Finally, formerly of the Forrest team, Michael Clark helped me describe the concepts found in the book.

This leads me to the final key acknowledgments. Two people had an unseen hand in this book. Both are gone now, but their advice and role modeling brought my two worlds together. The first was my grandfather of sorts by marriage, G. Allan Burton. Allan was the chairman of the Canadian retailer Simpsons. He became a role model because he was a veteran of the Second World War who served before and after the war in the Army Reserve. He modeled the ability to have a successful military career and a civilian career simultaneously. The other who influenced this book was my father, Christopher Chapman, an Academy Award–winning filmmaker. He never really understood my military focus, and while he would have preferred that I never joined the military, he always actively supported me. His advice was to not make a solo career out of the army; instead, he wanted me to ensure that I had a balance, which I did. I had one foot in the canoe and one on the shore. I had a successful part-time army career for thirty-four years and a civilian career simultaneously, retiring at the top of my army game as a brigadier general, which he just managed to see before he died.

Special thanks need to go to my family. My wife, Wendy, has supported me while putting up with a lot in our twenty-five years of marriage. As I worked two jobs simultaneously, she raised our four children while having a career of her own in the public sector. My kids have grown up used to Dad being away, whether on exercises or with clients. In these cases, my two eldest, Christopher and Amelia, never really saw their father. I suppose that has continued for the two youngest,

Robert and Alastair, who have not known my two careers yet have seen me out the door as the president of Forrest & Company as the business grows. They all supported me in these six months of book writing at home or at our cottage in the Thousand Islands, churning out the chapters.

As you read through the book, you will see the unseen hands of all these people and the others too numerous to acknowledge here.

INTRODUCTION

This book is about a journey and not a destination. Journeys are long affairs, and as you will see, this managerial leadership thing is a lifelong journey. My aim is to take you to the *center* of managerial leadership, to the core of what you and your organization really need.

For this book, I have relied on my experience of over thirty years personally leading leaders, then superimposing a simultaneous twenty-year career in leadership training and consulting. It is based in science and on the shoulders of many who have gone before me and paved the way.

In this time I believe that what leaders truly need is a way to manage the journey. On that trek you have to learn for yourself, and you learn as you go along. You need to take risks and be buffeted by both success and failure.

The analogy to journey I often refer our clients to is the epic poem *The Odyssey* by Homer. The story of the trials of Odysseus as he tries to get home and the challenges he faces once there is an analogy for all our lives. It is no different for the modern-day leader. It is an arduous journey, and if you as a leader are not growing (just like all living things), you are dying. This book is about that journey. Each of its chapters represents a milestone along the way. But no sooner do you get to the end than you have to start again. In the spirit of continuous improvement, you practice it throughout your professional life. Each situation and moment may look the same, but there is a learning from each. It truly is an expedition.

There is no shortcut or way around it. You have to keep going. As Winston Churchill said, "If you're going through hell, just keep going." It is the same on the managerial leadership journey. You must keep going forward, learning every moment along the way. You must face the challenges and risks in the same way. Our job as leaders is to meet those challenges and manage the risks for our people. In our society we have lost sight of the old military adage of mission, men (people), and me. Instead, it has been replaced with me, mission, and then the people.

That is why this book is an unconventional business pursuit. Too many businesses have lost sight of the importance of managerial leadership. I see lots of different organizations in my civilian career. There are many different sectors, and I am not a master of any one. Instead, the one common denominator for all organizations regardless of size or sector is people. We aren't at that stage yet where all human beings have been replaced by machines, so I am still safe with my claim. In my experience in the military, we had a phrase that denoted the difference between the army and the Royal Canadian

Navy. In the army we equip the man (or person), and in the navy we man the equipment. Regardless, in both of those, the common denominator was the human being. So whether your business is about technology or knowledge work, the same model applies.

What so many get wrong is that they see business as dollar signs. This is the conventional business pursuit. They become masters at managing those dollar signs, but they miss the human element. Dollars are made and lost by the people. The missing ingredient is the holistic managerial leader who brings the people together to achieve the objectives.

The argument that I make and that you will see unfold in this book is that, because of the common human element, there is a need for a *professionalism* in how we deal with people. It matters not whether it is in the work space or in the battlespace—we need a professional management corps.

It was not a fleet of fancy that I got into corporate leadership development with an army background. While every human is different, what they need is not. Leadership in business is the same as in the military and vice versa. That may be difficult to swallow given the nature of Hollywood's representation of the life in the military. What distinguishes the two types of businesses is their orientation to profit and nonprofit. Business is about profit and how to capitalize on it. The military is about how to deliver the national strategy. My perspective after over twenty years in business and thirty-four years serving in the military is that the two are not that different. The difference is actually within strategy. What has been clear in both of my careers is the need for us to *professionalize* managerial leadership. It isn't part of *other* work for those in management; it is the *key* to their work. The farther up you go in your career, the more true this becomes.

My earliest seminal case of training leaders in the army was while running a program that prepared leaders to engage in combat with thirty vehicles and three hundred troops and how to exercise control under high pressure and stress. Candidates in the program came from all walks of life. Some were the keen I've-got-this-in-the-bag types and some were the shy shrinking violets. Neither style mattered when the chips were down. Some bred greater confidence at the outset and others proved themselves in the crucible by their example. Years later at the army staff college, I taught thousands of troops more of the intellectual side of how to plan operations. The two constructs represent leadership and management, respectively.

From this I have turned my attention and that of our business to what business needs. So on the one hand, I focus on helping leaders to determine and express who they are, why they are here, and what they are trying to build, to the other extreme of figuring out where they want to be in the market and how to organize their employees to get there. Again, it is the connection of management and leadership regardless of experience.

The reason technical experience didn't matter was that it was more about the human condition. I can say that I have worked with so many industries and corporations that I am gradually getting a 360-degree view of business. I can now share valuable insights from one to the other. As I have always said, you have the answers in your own organization; we just have the questions to help the answers come out. You will get a sense of those questions in each chapter here. To help you move forward, I have set up questions to launch your thinking and propel you on the journey.

The real difference between organizations is strategy and not the human condition. It is about where organizations intend to be that defines them and not the common denominator of human beings who move the organization forward. Many have failed to realize that. What makes human beings special in their organizations does not change. The challenging part is that they are complex creatures, all with different needs and desires. This becomes the free radical that creates the complexity. Employees endeavor to be successful; they by and large give their best game in exchange for their paycheck. I believe this truth to be self-evident, that everyone is trying to be happy and do their best. Sometimes these two are at odds with each other. This is why the mission of Forrest & Company is to create great places to work that also achieve the strategy. The difference is one of strategy. What is the organization endeavoring to achieve, and is the workforce in congruence with it?

The problem here is that they are changing who they are or changing their strategy to fight an elusive ninja they can't see. In other cases, they cannot articulate their strategy, so no wonder the workforce cannot get behind it. Each is a failure of strategy, not of the employees. If the strategy is in congruence with the workforce, that is easy. They will measure the business based on their congruity with each other. If it is not, then it is a matter of leadership. Can you inspire them either individually or organizationally to follow the strategy?

If you are going to lead others to follow your strategy, you need to define it and then you need to expend your energy to lead the people to it. These are the two sides of management and leadership, and as you will see in the next chapter, they are inextricably linked. To do this, though, you need to be a professional and devote time and energy to your journey, continuously improving to be the best that you can be.

As you read through this book, recognize that there are a multitude of experiences and sources for the various thoughts that follow. I have relied on two seminal resources for my perspectives that you will read here. The first is about better thinking, *Conceptual Toolmaking: Expert Systems of the Mind* by Jerry Rhodes, and the second is a compendium of all facets of managerial leadership: *Requisite Organization: A Total System for Effective Managerial Organization and Managerial Leadership for the 21st Century* by Elliott Jaques.

So prepare yourself for the journey that will be the most satisfying and enlightening one you can possibly undertake. Leading and managing others fulfills our basic need of connection with others. When the journey is done and you can see that you have had a positive impact on those around you, you will know that you have truly lived the best of all lives.

CHAPTER 1

MANAGERIAL LEADERSHIP: THE FOUNDATION OF AN EFFECTIVE ORGANIZATION

The skills of managerial leaders separate successful organizations from unsuccessful ones.

I was nineteen years old when I underwent my first leadership training program. I had seen examples of bad leadership, and in the arrogance of youth, I thought I could do better. I thought I wanted to be a leader to make sure that no one had to experience the same bad leadership I had when I was a young private in the army. Well, I learned a lot of things on that first course, and now, almost forty years later, I am still learning. First, I learned that what was billed as leadership training was what one might refer to as management training. The second thing I learned was that I actually still had a lot to learn. That this thing we called leadership is a lifelong learning. In fact, it is a *craft*. The third thing I learned was that I was on a leadership path. I began to realize that the business of leading is hard work.

Words Hold Power

Managerial leadership is a bit of a mouthful, but I am using it as a term to provide clarity. Clarity is an issue for many of us. The reason, as my friend and mentor Jerry Rhodes says, is that "words are analogies for thought." While we think we may be using the same language, we may be thinking about the words very differently. The one I love to point to in organizations is the term *strategy*. To some, it means a grand strategy like Napoleon Bonaparte referred to, to others it is planning, and to still others it is a way to make you look important: "I'm developing the strategy for …" This confusion over the word leads to untallied wasted time as people argue about whether there is a strategy, if the strategy has changed, or that no one is following the strategy.

To a lesser extent, the words *management* and *leadership* also suffer from a lack of clarity. To compound this, we are judgmental about these words and ascribe a value to them. As an nineteen-year-old, I judged that the two words were mutually exclusive. Management had a pejorative description; it conjured up boring bureaucrats with tight ties who pore over spreadsheets and have little humor. Leaders, on the other hand, are seen as heroes—those who step out and save old ladies from being crushed by buses, or those who inspire millions with their daring charisma. Many of the business books that are written go to great lengths to decry management and exalt leadership. So, as we see the words on paper, we need to ask ourselves, What do we think about these words, and what speaks to our value set? Being a leader often is conflated with being out front. In that vein, it gets overused to describe fast runners or corporations in the marketplace. People bristle at being called managers. They want to be described as leaders. Even the military refuses to use the term, preferring to stick to the time-honored leader. The intent here is to demonstrate that, despite what countless business books say, leadership is not all there is, and management is not a bad thing. For me, this was a lesson that was not evident at first.

In the complexity of today's society, I believe we need each of them. We must embrace and utilize both for the betterment of our organizations and our world. As words are important, let me share my own definitions. Management is the act of administering an organization to make it efficient, effective, and trust-enhancing. Its orientation is to task delivery or output. I define leadership as the act of influencing, motivating, and enabling others to the achievement of tasks. Its orientation is toward people. They are indeed two different things. However, to be successful, you need them both. Too often, because of our prejudice for the word *management*, it has been overlooked. If you focus solely on leadership, you cannot guarantee success either. When I was nineteen, I was taught the importance of leadership and what leadership was supposedly about. In retrospect, it was how to manage weapon systems, navigate terrain, and coordinate people on a battlefield. By my definition, it was management and not about how to motivate, engage, and deal with people. The army had just made it all one thing, and that was leadership. They knew that management was important. They just didn't like the word.

MANAGEMENT
- The act of administering an organization to make it effective, either personally or through others
- Hard, tangible and focused on planning and process

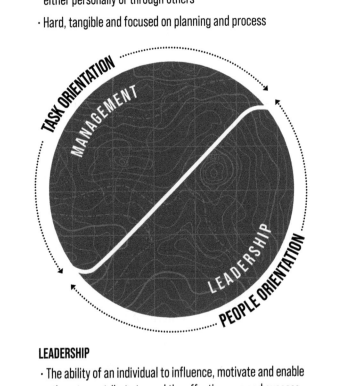

LEADERSHIP
- The ability of an individual to influence, motivate and enable others to contribute toward the effectiveness and success of the organizations of which he or she is a member
- Soft, intangible and focused on connecting with others and engaging them

Putting these constructs together, they become *managerial leadership*, which I define as the achievement of goals while having a positive impact on others. This new term ensures that they are both in play equally, rather than dividing them into separate competencies. To be successful, you need to focus on the task *and* the people. You need to balance being a taskmaster *and* a cruise director. If you focus only on management, you will drive people into the ground. If you are too pleasing and are focusing on everyone being excited or comfortable, you may not achieve the goal. It's important to balance the two and manage the tension between them.

In my experience, the key to managing the dichotomy of task and people begins with awareness. We often are not aware of our natural tendencies. Sometimes we get feedback in a multi-rater 360-degree feedback tool, or in other cases, someone tells us directly. In those cases, it is important to take the time to pause and reflect. Time and again those who have

> I have seen many a leader improve their game overnight by taking the time to pause, reflect, and make a choice. It is within us all to be the leader we choose to be.

paused and reflected have been able to change their approach. But it starts with that initial pause in the hurly-burly world we live in. I have seen many a leader improve their game overnight by taking the time to pause, reflect, and make a choice. It is within us all to be the leader we choose to be.

Managing the Tension

Tension is critical to success. As we like to say, tension seeks resolution. We need goals that pull us forward; otherwise, we don't go far enough. Think back to grade school and stretching an elastic band. If there was no tension, the elastic band never hit your classmate. We need the tension. It is healthy, and it is always present in the realm of tasks and people. Too many times in my career as a managerial leader, I let that tension go, usually in favor of the people and not the task. I see it all the time with clients: "I can't give that work to them; they have too much on their plates." That is not managing the tension. Instead, to quote William Oncken and Donald Wass, that is "putting the monkey on your back."[1]

The term *managerial leadership* expresses this tension. It also clarifies what type of leadership we are talking about. Far too many times when talking with clients or when we are preparing workshops on managerial leadership issues, there is confusion over the word *manager*. We hear, "These managers have no direct reports, and these leaders don't either." Our human penchant for labeling things (again, words have meaning) creates confusion. So it is useful to think in terms of managerial leadership. Many go so far as to suggest that leadership is a subset of the management function, but I suggest it's better to keep the notion of the two terms in balance and not think of one as being more important than the other. At

---

1   William Oncken Jr. & Donald L Wass, "Management Time: Who's Got the Monkey?" *Harvard Business Review* (November–December 1999): 1–7.

the risk of cultural appropriation, it is essentially a yin and yang construct without the light or dark side. But better still, I find it useful to go to root words and integrate from the Latin *integro*, which means "to make whole or restore." You make it whole by bringing the task and the people together. You must balance them and restore an equilibrium here.

The Impact of Our Experience

But it is not just the words that keep us from integrating these things. It is our experience and how we *see* managerial leadership. When we start our careers, we choose a profession whether as an electrician, accountant, lawyer, or other. Our early career is then set in motion on a path to being a technocrat of our profession, and our successes come at the hands of being a good accountant or code writer by fulfilling the tasks of that role. But as time goes on and we become more successful in our roles, we find we are still limited to our level of technical skills. Therefore, if we want to grow and be given more responsibility, we need to take on a managerial leadership role. In that role, we are now instead required to deliver results through others. The problem is that our foundation consists of the skills we have learned in our profession: we can always fall back on them.

> If we want to grow and be given more responsibility, we need to take on a managerial leadership role.

This is particularly prevalent in new managerial leaders. They have the foundation of their success that arises from their superior and now-recognized professional skills, and these anchor them and in a sense also make them feel whole. In other words, the perception is that their value consists of their experience and skills. What happens is that we don't fully understand that our work has changed. It is not only my task orientation but also the integration of those tasks with other people. You might begin to see where problems start to occur. I may not agree with how others do it because that is not my way or experience of doing it. I become a taskmaster quite quickly. If it is beyond my ken, I may recede from it and just be the cruise director and leave it to others. Either of these options is viable, but they belie the fact that my work has changed.

If we don't realize that it has changed, then when we don't get success out of others (the leadership side), we can easily turn to being taskmasters and begin driving task delivery (the management side). When this, too, fails, we drop into thinking, *Oh hell! I'll just do it myself.* When that anchor of our profession comes into play, we revert, and we get the job done personally. In my experience, this is the same model throughout industry and business regardless of sector. In fact, we feel pride that we added value by adding our professional skills to the task.

It is rooted in the fact that we feel lost without our technocratic skills. In effect, we have nothing to lean on. This, however, is not the reality. The real cause is that we don't value the profession of managerial leadership. Instead, we hang on to outdated industrial-era beliefs that we are valuable only if we can put a shoulder behind the wheel. We see ourselves as the technocrat and not as what we are truly being paid to be—someone who gets results through others while positively impacting them.

Our technocratic skills make us feel whole, and they give us comfort. A case in point would be the senior vice president of human resources who loved to close the door and pore over compensation spreadsheets. He felt like he was adding value in this way rather than focusing on his role as a managerial leader. We must realize that there needs to be a **profession of**

managerial leadership. There are professions of everything else. But for some reason, we see managerial leadership as something to be done on the side of the desk while we do our real functional work. This is why so many managers in leadership positions complain about all the human resources tasks they have to engage in.

The Profession of Managerial Leadership

The real reason managerial leadership is a distinct profession is that it requires lifelong learning and practice to integrate tasks and people. We can't behave as arrogant nineteen-year-olds and think we know it all. Nor can we be the person who takes one course and then thinks that the I-did-the-course box is checked. Sure, this is easy for me to say, as I have devoted my life to it. But trust me, the playing field is always changing. Realize that experience will not last forever and that our task skills will ultimately be redundant. If you doubt me, ask yourself how many people had experience with a global pandemic the likes of COVID-19.

> Thinking is the ultimate diversity, and what this means is that everyone sees the same thing, but they process it differently.

The other reason the profession of managerial leadership is lifelong is that it involves people. Every person is different. Thinking is the ultimate diversity, and what this means is that everyone sees the same thing, but they process it differently. Their biases come to the forefront. There is no cookie-cutter approach to human beings. They will always amaze you with their moments of individualism just as shockingly as they do with their moments of collectivism. If you think this is a one-and-done course, you are sadly mistaken. And a word to the wise here. If you don't value people, get out of the managerial leadership kitchen because managerial leadership is all about people. Do yourself and them a big favor and be an individual contributor instead. You can't fake it; they will sense it. It doesn't mean you can't be an introvert. You just have to value people. There is no hard-and-fast rule that extroverts win in the managerial leadership game. In both introversion and extroversion, in their true sense, they are about the individual and where they get energy. Managerial leadership is not about you yourself; it is what is necessary for your role.

Changing Mindsets

So how to solve for this? There is a way, but it requires several things to be in place. First, in our own psyche, we must realize that we can no longer lean on those basic technical skills that got us here. We need a new mindset, which is, *When I am in a managerial role,* that *is my work.* To do that, we also need a new skill set. We must realize that we need to learn new things and, most importantly, that those are managerial leadership skills. This learning as a managerial leader needs to be *your* learning, though. There is no silver bullet or magic vaccination to make you good at this. Both management and leadership skills *can* be learned. Too many times, people believe you have to be born with these abilities. This is not true. But to learn it, you need to first commit to it as a path.

There are three skills you must hone if you make this commitment. You need to first commit to reflect on and think about this new profession of yours. Reflection is not easy in the modern era. We live in the VUCA world, a term coined by the US Marine Corps. It stands for volatile, uncertain, complex, and ambiguous. I would argue that what makes reflection difficult is the speed of change as well as what I call the tyranny of do. The tyranny of do is the desire to be *doing things* rather than *thinking*. The tyranny of do is everywhere, and it pulls us to act as quickly as possible and not spend time reflecting. Whatever may be the cause that stops you from thinking, you need to commit to contemplating and learning.

The second skill that you need to acquire is discipline— that single-minded approach to stick to it. You will need the discipline to reflect in the face of VUCA and the tyranny of do. We lack discipline in modern society because we want a quick solution. For example, it is easier to take a pill to lose weight than to avoid a piece of chocolate cake.

Finally, the last skill you need to hone is to be yourself. I have hundreds of books on leadership and management, but I have to reflect and be disciplined to think it through rather than relying on the secret that someone may give me. Years ago, people followed the success of great generals like Welling-ton or Napoleon, but they weren't actually them. Corporations spend millions following some theory that was built in a different business with nothing to do with their own as the quick fix to solve their problems, such as Six Sigma, Kaizen, Lean, or, recently, Agile. Although all have their merits, realize that they are not derived from your business or from you, and while they might reduce risk, they are not of your body or your organization.

Universal Truths

This is to set a path consisting of eternal and universal truths to help you to achieve and maintain a high level of managerial leadership. Not a flavor of the month. Too often theories are developed to steer us away from the imperfect application of managerial leadership. The rise of leadership as all-important in business was a result of management practices that saw people as nothing more than human resources to be managed. In the 1950s environment, people saw others as resources to be controlled. The reaction to this was to label management as a bad thing. In effect, they threw the baby out with the bathwater. They had lost sight of the tensions and the need to integrate them, and as a result, management became a dirty word.

We must commit to the discipline to continuously improve ourselves. This shift in mindset and skills is not

> Managerial leadership is a lifelong learning–there is no one technical training course to take to achieve that designation.

easy. Managerial leadership is a lifelong learning—there is no one technical training course to take to achieve that designation. Instead, you continually build it up, and if you happen to be a perfectionist, beware—you will make mistakes. As both a practitioner and a teacher of managerial leadership for forty years, I have made thousands of mistakes, but in the lens of continuous improvement, I have learned from each one of them along the way.

On top of changing your mindset and your skill set, you need to seek help. There is one key role in the organization that is there to help you. Often we turn to human resources to help—and help you they can—but the one role you must rely on is your *manager*. They, too, will struggle with the same challenges, but their job is to help you. That is what managerial leadership is about: your manager is there to help you, not with the technical details but with the messiness of managerial leadership. Since it is a lifelong learning, they are on the same development path as you. They have even less chance to rely on their technical skills. They are getting farther and farther from the *doing* and more and more engaged in the *planning* and *thinking*. So it is important for you to reach out and to rely on one another. When your employees see this, they will become heartened that the management team is a productive, cohesive unit—a *managerial leadership* team.

So what does it matter what we call it?

It's because words do hold power. It is time for us to see the value in the work that we do by identifying it properly. It is sometimes challenging, can be frightening, and often does not bring immediate satisfaction, but it is important work. It is about carefully balancing management and leadership. It is also about realizing that, when you have direct reports, your work now is managerial leadership above all else. You need to change your mindset and your skill set, and you need to seek help where you may not have before. Your world has changed and continues to change. You need to adapt to be successful.

Managerial leadership is a mouthful. Now that you can see it as the integration of management and leadership, when you see the words *manager* or *leader*, you will know it is emphasizing the task or the people side—but remember, to be successful, you need to integrate them.

Milestone #1: Reflect On and Consider the Nature of Management and Leadership

Welcome to the first milestone on your journey. Milestones were originally what the Romans used to mark distance on their roads. Since then, it has come to mean a stage in development. So our first stage in the journey is to reflect on and consider the nature of management and leadership, not only in ourselves but also in others. The next chapter will set us up to see just what needs to happen to create a profession of managerial leadership for your organization.

On a scale of 1 to 10, what level of integration do you see at your organization between management and leadership?

What are the reasons for this, in your view?

What should be done?

What is your own attitude toward the words management and leadership?

Where does that come from?

What will you do about this?

What is your orientation toward tasks or people?

Why?

How does this manifest itself?

What does your manager value, task or people?

What are the implications?

What must you do?

What does your organization value, orientation to task or people?

What are the implications?

What might you do?

How well do you balance between task and people or management and leadership?

How do you know?

What are the implications?

CHAPTER 2

MANAGING MANAGERS

The force multiplier of organizational success is aligned management.

A client company we worked with some years ago was led by a brilliant CEO; she was charismatic, cared for her people, and had developed a clear strategy as to what she wanted the business to grow up to be. The problem was that when you asked levels further down what this strategy meant, they were confused. A simple statement that "the business needed to sing" was lost at the lower levels when people were asking when the singing lessons would begin and when they were getting pianos. The problem wasn't the employees; it was the strategy that was lost in translation. The insight from this dilemma was an important part of my journey in the realm of managerial leadership. I realized that the key to organizational success was in fact the manager of managers' or the leader of leaders' role. The managerial leaders were not making the strategy *real* to their people, and the cascade was ignored in favor of a stove-piped message.

Managerial Leadership Is the Universal Translator

The key to organizational success is leading leaders or managing managers. No matter where you are in the organization, the success really does come from your boss. This statement may rankle you right now. Many of those business books out there tell you it is all about the employee, and yes, they are right, but in business, government, ecclesiastical groups, and nonprofits, the business really does require the bosses to be the drivers.

One of the pieces related to our question of why we don't practice managerial leadership is that we don't value the role of being bosses. I have seen time and time again that many individuals in managerial leadership roles do not value telling people what to do. These are sometimes deep-seated beliefs that go back to what Mom and Dad taught them, or they are their own value sets. But as bosses, we have a role to play, and that includes telling people what to do. If we combine not valuing that aspect of the work with a sense that we are technocrats, we can see why our people and our teams aren't as successful as they could be. And if they are successful, it is not because we were good bosses.

In our work at Forrest & Company, we have compiled years of research on organizational pain points. We have gathered this information through workshops to help make the organization more effective. Organizational pain nags at people. To get back to stasis without pain, the organization, like humans, needs to burn energy to get back in order. But just as the human body burns energy to deal with stressors, there comes a point when the energy is used up, our resilience becomes low, and we succumb. Organizational pain is like that: If left to get worse, it can be debilitating. Our job as consultants is to help organizations reduce the pain to deliver the strategy.

The strategy is the *all* in every organization. Although culture can eat strategy for breakfast, we exist inside the organization to deliver the strategy. Again, it doesn't matter whether you are in the private sector, public sector, or nonprofit sector. We are all there to deliver the strategy. This can be problematic if we don't have a strategy, or if it is unclear, or if it is just created in an executive

> The strategy is the all in every organization. Although culture can eat strategy for breakfast, we exist inside the organization to deliver the strategy.

session and never referred to again. These are all things that make the lives of managerial leaders very difficult. So determining the pain and endeavoring to remove it is crucial to organizational effectiveness. This is a critical managerial role for our managerial leaders.

Common Organizational Pain

Based on our research, we have identified eleven organizational pain points as recognized by managers. See if these reflect your organization:

* **MANAGERIAL INEFFECTIVENESS:** "Our employees feel … unclear / not respected / over- or undersupervised / directionless / unsure of who really is their boss."

* **UNPRODUCTIVE MEETINGS:** "There are too many meetings with too many people or the wrong people, with too few constructive outcomes."

* **LACK OF TRUST:** "There's too much politics. Unmet expectations have made us suspicious or resentful of each other."

* **LACK OF DECISION-MAKING:** "Decisions take too long." "We're stuck in analysis paralysis in a culture of risk aversion and fear of failure."

* **RESOURCE SQUABBLES:** "We have to fight for the support we need from other departments or just to get the resources to do our jobs."

* **WORK OVERLOADING:** "The work keeps piling up. We don't know why we're doing it or what good it's doing. We're not even sure that it's our work. It is never-ending."

* **INEFFECTIVE POLICIES:** "Our policies and processes are outdated and are getting in the way of getting the job done."

❋ **LACK OF INNOVATION:** "There is a lack of innovation and creativity in our organization. New ideas never move forward. Opportunities to improve productivity are lost. We seem hidebound."

❋ **GENERAL INEFFECTIVENESS:** "The projects and initiatives we launch come in late and/or over estimated resources."

❋ **POOR STRATEGY AND IMPLEMENTATION:** "We continually miss our quarterly goals." "Our strategy doesn't make sense."

❋ **LACK OF TALENT:** "We don't have the right talent for the work we have."

Whenever I show this list to groups, they generally relate to two or more. We have also surveyed human resources professionals and asked which they considered to be the ones that impact employees the most. **Overloading came out on top, followed by managerial ineffectiveness and unproductive meetings.** Not surprisingly, there is no time to reflect and think; we live and work within the tyranny of do. That managerial ineffectiveness is in the top three indicates again a lack of a professional managerial leadership approach. Additionally, during COVID-19, this overloading has only grown astronomically as a major pain point and issue. As one client said during the pandemic, "I no longer work at home; instead, I am sleeping at my office."

After we have amassed details of a team's pain and we share the preceding list, there are a couple of aha moments. The first is that other businesses aren't so different from us. It becomes proof to the old adage that the grass isn't greener on the other side of the fence. Your competitors probably have the same problems you have.

Then we ask, "Why is there common pain?" This is when the crowd goes strangely quiet. The common pain comes from the nature of organizations, and therefore there is an inescapability to this. The nature of the human condition in organizations creates a similarity across organizations. That doesn't mean we should give up; instead, it means we should redouble our efforts to reduce the pain.

The Doctor Manager

The burning question, though, is, Whose problem is it anyway? After pondering and reflection, a team usually concludes that it is "our problem" as the organization's leadership. So instead of trying to rewrite managerial leadership into self-directed teams or workgroups, the energy needs to be spent in resolving this pain because it won't go away without radical relationship changes. It needs the steady hand of managerial leaders to reduce the pain. It can't be left to the employees to solve this pain. This is the real work of managerial leaders. So the issue is laid squarely on the managerial leaders. After all, if the pain exists in the first place, it has only been exacerbated because of poor management. If we don't believe that reducing pain is our work as managerial leaders, how can we expect the pain to dissipate? The fads discussed throughout management books miss the point that the role of managerial leadership is to enable our people to deliver the task while having a positive impact.

Strategy Is Your North Star

The starting point to remove this pain is being a professional managerial leader. But there is a challenge in the environment that managerial leaders work within. What do I take on so that I am not Don Quixote tilting at windmills? This brings us back to the issue of strategy, because strategy defines what is important. As I mentioned earlier, lack of clarity causes huge pain for organizations and for their people as well. It is a pain point that comes up frequently—poor strategy and execution. Of the top four pain points for CEOs, not hitting our goals is one of the big ones. (The others are lack of an engaged workforce, lack of innovation, and we aren't taking care of the customer.) These are two sides of the same coin. Their roots are ill-defined strategy, strategy lost in translation, or strategy not being followed. **The strategy is the guidebook of the organization.** It defines what we want to be and what is important. What is important is critical to decision-making. It defines what we need and what we want. It defines what good looks like as an end state but not as a means to get there. The thinking that goes into this type of strategy is very different from planning. In my strategy definition, you assess your work and determine where you want to be. You do this by using your imagination to plan the analysis, evaluation, and interpretation. Too often organizations and particularly

C-suites lose sight of this. The corporate off-site meetings enable you to get away and reflect, but all too often, that is where it ends. We all leave satisfied that we had a good chat. Driving the strategy day-to-day is what counts. For strategy to be effective, it needs follow-through. The strategy points the way for the organization and for the endeavors and aspirations of all the people within it.

> **Driving the strategy day-to-day is what counts.**

I describe our Forrest & Company strategy work as helping clients to articulate their strategy and then aligning the organization behind it. Articulating the strategy defines their vision, their mission, their values, and their purpose as well as their key goals. It is to make decisions in these realms, and executive teams need to explore their strategic drivers, their value chain, and their sustainable competitive advantage. Exploring these two thinking clusters is essential to get the organization behind the strategy. This work is managerial work. It is necessary for the success of the business. Without it, all the greatest leadership traits in the world will not get you where you want and need to be. Aligning the organization behind the strategy requires not only leadership skills but also management skills. It is no good standing up as a leader calling, "Once more into the breach." You need to consider what to do to reinforce that direction of the North Star. Your work needs to be to plan and organize. This is just the starting point. Once the plans are in place, you can rely on leadership to engage with your people, but if you have not done the groundwork, you will merely anger them by giving them more work and leading them into endless meetings as they try to figure out how to deliver the strategy. Hence you get people trying to ascertain how many pianos they will need and who sings best.

Create the Sandbox

Aligning the organization isn't about team building and trust falls. Too often we work on solving behavioral issues with team building. It's a good business for us, but it is not the issue. In our experience, the real trick is to build the team, not team build. Building the team is about aligning the team. Aligning is about clarifying who does what and what support they can expect to achieve their work. It is about defining their sandbox, ensuring they have room to maneuver in it, and providing all the toys (resources) they need to succeed in that sandbox. In the early days of empowerment, we let people go in the belief that they would naturally find their way and would be more engaged. We didn't build sandboxes; instead, we launched them into the Sahara. So they quickly became lost, and what is more, they had no idea who would be there to help them. Aligning the organization is all about creating structure for people to work together effectively. A client of ours called it the freedom of structure. This can appear to be an oxymoron. It is profoundly releasing to give me my sandbox, as it gives me a place to stand that fits my capability, and from there I can move the world. Too often we don't spend the time to structure the work, and we leave it to our employees to figure out, which leads to pain. The most probable outcome is that we don't deliver the strategy, and soon we all have problems.

By now, if you are keeping a tally, you can already see that a lot of managerial leadership work is coming to you. Because regardless of your level in the organization, your work is to define those sandboxes. If you don't value this work, it is problematic, and if you don't have the time because you are too busy reading spreadsheets, then that, too, is problematic. You can expect the pain points previously mentioned and even more that haven't been addressed. At this point, when

> **Regardless of your level in the organization, your work is to define those sandboxes.**

I am in workshops explaining this, I often start to get pushback, such as "We don't have time for this." This is probably true if you are doing what you usually do. The key here is that you as a managerial leader need to get really good at delegating. By delegating, I don't mean dumping but rather delegating all those things that are at the level of capability of your direct reports. To do that, you need to practice the golden rule of leadership: Know your people and promote their welfare. Don't delegate those things that are at your level of capability. Know their skills, experience, attitude, and confidence toward the task you need to delegate.

Those still struggling with what they thought was their work now realize they have this extra work too. I suggested earlier that there is a role that can help you through these challenges. That is your boss. Now, before you react in horror at the prospect of that particular boss helping you, I need you to be a bit theoretical for a moment. This book is designed for a particular set of managerial leaders, and as we go on, I intend to provide you with the tools to be successful. The real pain points in organizations do not emanate from the frontline managerial leaders. Of course, they can contribute to it, but it falls squarely at the feet of their bosses and their bosses' bosses. To manipulate and modernize a quote from arguably the greatest British general of the Second World War, Field Marshal Viscount Slim of Burma, "There are no bad organizations, only bad managerial leaders." It isn't the organization's fault, and it can't be solely "those guys down there." The adage that the fish rots from the head is very true, and it rots as it travels down.

An organization's pain is at the feet of the director level and above. If our bosses of bosses are not professional managerial leaders, then how can we expect anyone below them to be? To be clear, though, there are very few business books dedicated to this topic. Instead, we lump leadership books into the realm of dealing with people, so they are generic. But once you add the managerial side, they can no longer be generic. This is what is necessary in organizations—the clarity of what bosses of bosses do and how it is different. But back to reality for a moment. If you recoiled in horror about getting help from that boss, realize that in this framework, it isn't that boss's problem that they are ineffective and cannot help you.

It is the problem of your boss's boss that they are not being led and managed effectively. This is an important watershed in understanding the nature of managerial leadership. It must be functioning throughout. It is about ensuring that people get the leadership they need to be successful at all levels.

Linking Strategy to the Work

The final element to define the importance of managing managers or leading leaders is to realize that the middle of the chain is the linking pin. Our role in managing managers is to link our leaders with the strategy. But that linking pin creates a tension. That tension is between what we call Team One and Team Two. Team One represents your boss's team. It consists of you among your peers. Team Two is you as the leader of your direct reports. These are numbered this way because Team One is your first priority. You have to be a member of your boss's team first before you can lead Team Two. In other words, you have to be a follower before you can be a leader. Too often this relationship gets messed up. If I am focused on Team Two first, I will not necessarily cooperate with my peers. I will go to a meeting with my Team One peers and then return to my Team Two and say, "This isn't what I think; this is what they want ..." This is classic Team Two first thinking. In Team One, we gain alignment so that we know how to play the game together. Once we have alignment in Team One, we earn the right to lead Team Two.

Lateral Integration and Vertical Execution

A simple way to remember this is lateral integration before vertical execution. In Team One, we laterally integrate—we understand how we fit together, what each of our roles are, and what the expected behavior is—and then we vertically execute on that in Team Two. We call this the LIVE model because we live in two teams: Team One and Team Two. Whenever I share this with an executive team, the lights go on. They suddenly realize how those silos got created in the first place. They vertically executed without laterally integrating. For the executive, first achieving lateral integration in Team One is critical. As one wag put it, if you get this backward, you get EVIL.

Not all of us can accept this framework immediately. I remember when, as a Battalion Commander, I announced this framework to my company commanders, who were all very bright and excellent officers. They were hard chargers and really were smarter than me. They did not take well to this idea that they had to follow Team One first. However, when I swung it back on them and asked, "Do you not expect your leaders to be laterally integrated before they set out?" they all agreed. The model is situational; sometimes we are the employee, sometimes the manager, and sometimes the managers once removed. It all depends on the lens through which you look at these things. Many times in my career, I haven't been a great follower. This is a burden I carry with me, but it is also clear to me that it is essential if the strategy is to be achieved. Sometimes we have a boss who doesn't add value to our work, and they make it hard to be a follower. But as I say to my coaching clients in those predicaments, we have a choice. That choice is to decide just how much you will put up with before cutting bait and walking away.

Alignment Is a Key Managerial Leadership Role

Alignment to strategy is the work of the managerial leader. The employees can't make themselves aligned; they are following our lead. The problem for organizations is when we don't lead–and this is the issue for the directors and upward in organizations–the managers of managers or leaders of leaders. For if they do not focus on this critical role, the pain in the organiza-

> The problem for organizations is when we don't lead-and this is the issue for the directors and upward in organizations-the managers of managers or leaders of leaders.

tion becomes unbearable. The strategy is missed, and the organization falters. The mission fails, and a rot sets in to destroy the remnants.

If you are still struggling with this idea, fear not, for it will become clearer as we look at what is at the core of organizational success. It is interlinked with the role of the boss's boss and for that matter with the entire chain of human effort in the organization.

There is an adage in the army. Time spent on recce (reconnaissance) is seldom wasted. Looking around and figuring out where you are and what is going on is worth the time spent. Time spent on defining work and roles and connecting ourselves to the strategy will pay off in spades for you. It is within your realm of control. You can do it. Take the time and don't get caught in the tyranny of do. If you set aside the time to understand your pain and link your teams together, you will find that you can achieve so much more.

Milestone #2: Managing Managers

The next milestone on your journey is to consider the nature of your organization and your managers. Start yourself on the path to being the best manager of managers you can be by thinking through where you, your organization, its strategy, and your managers are at. In the next chapter, we will explore what makes it all work (the role of accountability) and how it can launch your and your organization's success. It becomes your unique sustainable competitive advantage.

What are the top three pain points in your organization?

What are the reasons for this, in your view?

What can you do about it?

How clear are you on the strategy?

What needs clarification?

How will you get greater clarity?

How clear are your managers on the strategy, and how is their work aligned to it?

Why is that?

What needs to be done?

How clear are your managers on their sandbox to work toward delivering the strategy?

Why is that?

How will you go about clarifying if need be?

How aligned are you with your manager's team?

How aligned are you with your own team?

Why is there a difference, and what will you do to change it?

How aligned are your managers to your team?

How do you, or will you, know?

If they are not, how will you get them there?

47

CHAPTER 3:

APPLICATION OF MANAGERIAL ACCOUNTABILITY: THE CORE OF SUCCESS

Accountability distinguishes the professional from the amateur.

The core of organizational success came to me later in life somewhat embarrassingly. It was a function of a reflection on failures and the insight of others. It wasn't quite a eureka moment, but rather it built up over time. As a leadership trainer, one gets professional pride from those moments when it clicks for participants. Whether it was windswept hills in pouring rain or air-conditioned classrooms, it comes at precisely that moment when participants are excited by what they have learned. They are motivated and ready to tilt at the windmills and to take that learning back to the workplace. The problem is that as you follow your prodigy, your sense of fulfilment and success is quickly dampened. I began to realize that I was pumping sunshine into them only to find that they were running into walls back at the office. Our society suggests that you can move mountains with good hard work, and that was not the case. What I learned was that Western societal values were flawed in a number of ways. I believed they could do anything. They just needed to be motivated. I learned that we were putting the burden on them to change the world. We posited it all on the individual to be the sole force of change. We were trying to make them committed to creating change in some kamikaze fashion. What was missing was a key ingredient—their boss. They needed a boss to help them to clarify and to coach and above all to point the way.

The problem with this training method was that we were relying on their sense of responsibility to take the learning and do something with it. This led me to become an advocate of accountability first and then responsibility.

Accountability: The Key to Success

Accountability is in the news. Pundits claim its lack as the cause of the Great Recession. CEOs call for it as the means to climb out of their economic doldrums. While all this talk is encouraging, it has contributed more to the mystification of accountability than to its clarity. As a result, intrigued executives, only lightly delving into accountability, often recoil.

As we discussed earlier, words have meaning, so it's time for a little definition work. We define accountability differently from responsibility, and while many books talk about the importance of accountability, few define it the way we do. Even if you go to the dictionary and look up the word *accountability*, you'll see that it says "see responsibility," and when you look up the word *responsibility*, it says "see accountability." But by following my definitions, I think you will see where organizational pain really stems from as well as all the other issues we have discussed so far. As Antoine de Saint-Exupéry noted in *The Little Prince*, *"Words are the source of misunderstandings."*[2]

By responsibility, we mean a subjective personal sense of commitment or obligation. In other words, *I feel* responsible to do something, to act in a certain way. In comparison, we define accountability as the objective component between a managerial leader and their direct report. A managerial leader holds their direct report accountable to do something. In responsibility, the onus is on the individual, whereas in accountability, the onus is on the boss. In my experience, though, while CEOs would like accountability, very few really understand it. Instead, organizations become responsibility-based. In other words, the onus is on the individual to be successful.

An analogy of responsibility came to me while watching my eight-year-old son playing soccer. If you have ever seen eight-year-olds play soccer, they are like bees—they swarm

---

2   Antoine de Saint-Exupéry, *The Little Prince* (New York: Reynal & Hitchcock, 1943).

the ball. In some cases (sometimes including my son), they pick flowers. In one case, there was a boy named Simon on the team. Simon's mom and dad had clearly taught Simon that good boys score and that players of the game are there to take that ball and score at all costs. This is the height of responsibility. The ones who are picking flowers merely have a lesser sense of responsibility, but Simon has a greater sense.

But if we rely solely on people's sense of responsibility, we are headed into problems, and it is these problems that plague organizations. The trouble is that responsibility is subjective. And not all of us are the same. We are diverse. We have different experiences and DNA. The distinction is that with accountability, just like with a professional soccer team, we all have a position to play, and when we score, we score

The key to accountability is consequences.

as a team. In turn that team can accept different senses of obligation as long as we meet the standard for the group. I apologize for a sports analogy, but the next time you read a book discussing accountability, ask yourself if they mean accountability or responsibility. Too many books try to use accountability to describe responsibility, but you cannot really hold yourself to account.

The key to accountability is consequences. Once again, words have power, so realize that in this context I mean both positive and negative consequences. Unfortunately, too often we focus on negative consequences. As a parent, I have spent far too much time on the negative side of consequences. Eventually I learned that, over time, children don't even hear it anymore. So I believe the real skill of a managerial leader is the search for the good. Focus on the positives, because then when you do apply a negative consequence, it has more impact.

Consequences are on a spectrum that you need to be adept at using. Too often managerial leaders are binary; positive is bonus and negative is firing. As a leader, you need to manage the spectrum. That spectrum has a midpoint. A verbal acknowledgment for a job well done or a congratulatory note are all positive. Discussion of how something could have been done better or sending a note to file are all on the negative side of the spectrum. Manage that spectrum through coaching and feedback. When you understand that this is the essence of coaching and feedback, it becomes less scary. The final point to bear in mind is that accountability is part of your job or your role. Consequence application is what you are accountable for, and if you don't execute, your boss needs to have the same accountability conversation with you and demonstrate the spectrum of consequences.

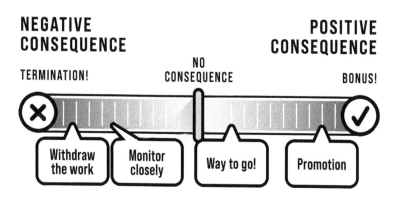

Make It Just about Work

Accountability is what makes things less personal and more about the role. It isn't about the exalted level I have achieved but rather about what my role is in delivering the strategy. Too much focus on the subjective, personal perspective has led to all sorts of issues in managerial leadership. However, it doesn't rest at the feet of that individual. It is at the feet of their boss for having allowed it to get to that state. Arguably, unchecked responsibility breeds hubris and arrogance, and accountability drives to the greater good. Often the cry goes up that accountability stifles creativity. This is furthest from the truth because accountability isn't about painting everything the same. It is about good managerial leadership, where you know your people and give them roles and tasks that engage them and their creativity within the sandbox walls. This is because the sandbox represents the role in relation to the strategy; it is not about being left in the Sahara.

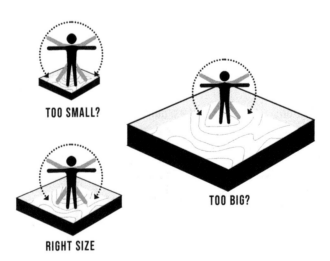

TOO SMALL?

RIGHT SIZE

TOO BIG?

Authority Bestowed

The final point on accountability is that it has an important sidekick, and only accountability can deliver it. The integral piece to accountability is authority. Authority represents legitimated power. Since responsibility is a personal feeling of obligation, there can be no clearly defined authority, as the authority lies in each individual. But in cases where there is only responsibility, then people will seize authority. In this case it is illegitimate power. It is a free-for-all when we grab for authority to fulfill what we believe is our role and achieve our goals. Consider the finance clerk who feels responsible to protect the business's finances. They feel they have to tell the executive vice president that they cannot claim that expense. Or, in my experience, the logistics clerk who refuses to ensure that troops get the kit they need because they are husbanding resources. These are all indicators of managerial leadership being abrogated. When we rely on responsibility, we have to live in policies and rules. Policies are designed to curb people's sense of responsibility, and because they often are based on past experience, they lack the flexibility to respond to new issues. They are wielded to provide roadblocks to flexibility as well as to remove it. In extremes, they are designed to control the 90 percent, based on the 10 percent who will do it anyway. Instead, organizations need to exercise accountability and hold those 10 percent who are "scoundrels" to account instead of constraining the 90 percent. These are simply more examples of the lack of managerial authority and managers of managers not doing their jobs. We need to give people the authority to succeed in their work through clarity—the clarity that only we as managerial leaders can give them.

Accountability without commensurate authority is unfair, and authority without accountability is dangerous, as we have just seen. Authority represents the legitimated power to make decisions and expend resources. The time organizations spend on these is crucial to organizational effectiveness. Having an accountability should represent the authority to make decisions in that realm. However, since most of the work in organizations is done laterally, what does that mean in relation to others? Too often we use terms like *ownership*. Ownership is a responsibility word, and in the cold light of day, unless you are the shareholder or the true owner-operator, you don't own it. Ownership is back to husbandry. It is often unclear what ownership means in the reality of day-to-day work. Is it the authority to make decisions, or does it mean you are expected to protect the work as though you owned the company—who knows? Imported management constructs such as RACI (responsible, accountable, consulted, and informed) from project management don't help either. Aside from having accountability and responsibility in the same framework, it only goes so deep. People need and desire clarity on their ability to control their accountabilities. What is required is

> Accountability without commensurate authority is unfair, and authority without accountability is dangerous.

careful thought about what is expected and what rights someone has to engage in the work.

Authority is not limited to just making decisions and expending resources. It also goes into the realm of getting service, calling meetings, and having a say in what others do outside your team. In other words, it is about carefully thinking through the work and, most importantly, how the work needs to be defined laterally. It is a function of lateral integration. Once you do this, you start to remove the silos that naturally occur.

In one particular case, I was working with the executive team of a multinational financial institution. I explained the need to carefully clarify the nature of authority of what the limits and extents were for the organization. Naturally, whether they felt threatened that I had suggested they were not doing their job or whether they truly believed it, they rejected it almost immediately. Their response was that it was impossible to define authority; it was too much work. For them it was probably true. It got in the way of their technocratic work, but they had condemned the organization to ambiguity and stress as everyone tried to make things work. They had abrogated their accountability as managerial leaders. They had missed a great engagement opportunity in their organization.

Authority Is a Very Human Desire

In my experience, people are often clear on their accountabilities for task or function (also known as their technocratic realm), but they are not clear on their authority. Clarity of authority reduces stress because I don't have to try to find the person who might help me; instead, I am clear on my ability to control their actions to achieve what I am accountable to deliver. Without this clarity, I have to rely on my personal relationships, which is the cachet to get things done in many organizations. I liken it to the backroom drug deals that are done to help me achieve my goals. If I have been in the organization for years, I might navigate this myriad of interpersonal relationships. However, the new members have no sense of how things are done here. Clarity of authority is what we crave.

The Power of Control

We as humans naturally crave authority because it represents our realm of control. Control is essential for our well-being. We live in a world that in most situations is outside our control. The CEO has the greatest sense of control but can be hemmed in by the board, just as the board is hemmed in by regulatory controls that will hold them ultimately accountable. At the lower levels of the organization where the real work is done, they have the least sense of control. Having a sense of not being in control can be very destabilizing. This is why in responsibility-based organizations, we try to seize control. It makes us feel whole. This lack of control requires us to burn energy and leads to stress casualties. In the role of managerial leaders, our job is to reduce this stress by knowing our people and promoting their welfare. It is not just a management role, as we are performing a leadership function to integrate the two.

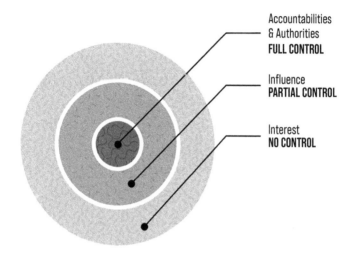

Accountabilities & Authorities
FULL CONTROL

Influence
PARTIAL CONTROL

Interest
NO CONTROL

Clarifying Control of Another Leader's Role

As leaders, we need to help our people to be clear on what they have full control over. They need to have a sense of their limits and extents. Can I expend this money? Can I make this decision? Can I give them a bonus? These are all elements of control that need clarifying. This full control represents their accountability and authority. We need to clarify where they have partial control. Partial control is where something is in the full control of someone else and I need to persuade them to my perspective. I have seen leaders who, when faced with this, back away time and again. We need to sell our thinking, and we need to help people to see our perspective. They will not naturally go there, so we need to find a way to get them there.

Finally, we have to help leaders understand the realm of their interest and realize that what lies in that realm is what they have no control over. They need to disregard this last realm. It brings nothing but emotional upheaval and angst. It has taken me a lot of time and reflection to realize the differences within these various realms. Too much of my energy has been lost in getting upset by the things in my sphere of interest. My time is better spent on where I have full control and where I can influence. This is where the interrelationship of accountability and responsibility comes back into focus. Without the parameters of accountability where I have full control, I will feel responsible for everything.

Accountability First, Then Responsibility

Before we leave this issue of responsibility, allow me to be clear: Responsibility is not a bad thing. Just as we took management and leadership apart and then brought them back together, we need to do the same with accountability and responsibility. Neither can exist without the other. It is, however, their emphasis that is important. When I used the example of training leaders, they were being left to their sense of responsibility to take on what they had learned. **They really needed the system of accountability and authority to make them successful.** You cannot have blind accountability without the personal commitment of responsibility. Once you give someone an accountability, there is an expectation that they are committed to it. This is the bond between manager and employee.

In the end, it is a matter of sequencing. Accountability must come before responsibility for complete success. To believe you can hold someone accountable without their sense of responsibility kicking in will lead to a standoff. It is a careful balance with the two halves coming together, and the glue that binds them is dialogue. It is useless for the manager to fly in, squawk, dump a bunch of stuff on them, and fly away. Instead, the leader in you must connect with them and engage in a dialogue by discussing the situation at hand. Dialogue by its nature represents a two-way conversation; it is not a monologue. You need to hear their concerns and issues. However, once they agree to a certain responsibility, you have to be prepared to apply accountability to hold them accountable and apply consequences both good and bad. In retrospect, this management approach of being the taskmaster who was busy dumping and running away gave management a bad name. But again, you have to manage the tension between the task and the person. That said, it is not the sole disconnection for managerial leaders. In our experience, the lack of clarity of what managers are accountable for in their own roles has impacted their effectiveness.

> In our experience, the lack of clarity of what managers are accountable for in their own roles has impacted their effectiveness.

The Real Work of Leaders: Their Accountabilities

As I mentioned earlier, we are clear on our accountabilities for function or tasks, but we are not clear on what our accountabilities are for managerial leadership. Time and again, when we do role clarity work, everyone is romanced by the stone of what their technocratic accountability is, but rarely are they interested in their accountability as managerial leaders. This lack of interest is where we begin to see where strategy fails—who is minding the shop and making it work? We need to realize that we must be clear on our accountabilities and authorities in our preeminent role of managerial leaders. Here is your test: Ask a manager what they are accountable for. The answer will inevitably be a technical accountability. Ask them their management accountabilities. In my experience, they struggle to see beyond the management of that technical skill. We as managerial leaders need to make our leaders aware.

THE FIRST ACCOUNTABILITY:
COMMITMENT TO THE WORK

For an organization to be truly effective, managerial leadership accountabilities preempt our technocratic accountabilities. Just as it is fundamentally unfair to have accountability without authority, these generic accountabilities have their commensurate authorities. The first cluster relates to the nature of all employees. **So the first accountability is that I must be committed to the work my manager gives me.** In turn the first authority of an employee becomes the accountability of a manager to ensure their rights are protected. Strangely enough, in exchange for a paycheck, employees are expected and therefore accountable to work with full commitment on the work assigned by their manager. As an accountability, they need to be held to account by their manager in order to work this way. There are some aspects of my job I don't like, but I am committed to the work, and my manager needs to exercise her judgment and discretion in assessing if I demonstrate commitment. In exchange for that, I need the authority to have the work expectations and resources clearly defined for me by her. **Therefore, to be protected, my first authority is to be safe physically.** I should not have to be worried that I am not safe, and I have the right to be protected by my boss. **The second authority I need is to be coached by someone more capable than me.** It now becomes the work of my leader to coach me or to find me a coach. The best organizations make it the leader's accountability to coach. There is a value to my boss coaching me and not outsourcing my development.

THE SECOND ACCOUNTABILITY: TO WORK AT THE LEVEL AT WHICH YOU ARE BEING PAID

Part of the accountability to work with full commitment is to work at the level of my role, not above it and not below it. If I am working above my role, I am doing someone else's work, and if I am below it, I am wasting resources. This accountability is really important for managerial leaders with a technocratic bent, as they need to be doing the work at the level they are being paid for. Too often managerial leaders drop down and do the work of their direct reports. It is my manager's job to ensure that I am working at the right level and also to ensure that I have the capability for it. If I don't, it is not my fault and it is instead hers, as she has put me in a sandbox too small or thrown me into the Sahara again.

THE THIRD ACCOUNTABILITY: BEST ADVICE AS THE ELIXIR OF ENGAGEMENT

The next accountability is absolutely mission critical to organizational success. It is the source of open and honest dialogue and changes the nature of engagement in organizations. **It is the game changer and creates a sustainable competitive advantage.** It is the third accountability, which is to give my manager my best advice. As part of my work, I give my manager my best ideas, recommendations, and suggestions. My manager will listen and consider the best advice and decide whether to act on it. Once again this is laden with actions by the manager. The manager needs to set up the conditions to enable me to feel comfortable. My commensurate authority for best advice is to be safe psychologically and socially. She will not embarrass me in front of my peers or belittle me and damage my self-esteem. **This authority goes beyond best advice because I need to be safe from intimidation and from being ostracized by others, and it is my manager's job to ensure that I am.** As you can imagine, if organizations had respected the right to be safe physically, psychologically, and socially, we would not have unions or a need for diversity, inclusion, and equity programs because managers would have been doing their jobs. We need to be clear: Best advice is not a responsibility; rather, it is an accountability. Not all of us will be comfortable giving best advice independently, but our managers must demand it using their best leadership skills. But a word of warning: As the manager, you need to park your ego. A CEO client of ours referred to this as putting on his tin hat. The best advice bullets were coming at him because of something he had or hadn't done. But if you are going to be a professional managerial leader, you need to harden yourself to it. It is a long journey to full implementation of best advice, but the fruits are well worth it.

THE FOURTH ACCOUNTABILITY: STAY WITHIN THE VALUES

Finally, my last employee accountability to my boss is to stay within the values of the organization. Values define what is good in an organization. Once again, my boss has work to do, and in many cases, the organization does as well. Values exercises are usually linked to strategy, and like strategy, they become dormant as a place mat or plaque on the wall. By holding me accountable to the values, you make them real. They need to be part of the performance evaluation system, just as these accountabilities all do. If they are measured, they will get done. Too often organizations create elaborate measures for performance evaluation, but they need to be based on the work you expect me to do and not on some competency model developed by others. Make them real and you will get the performance you need to deliver the strategy. The more disconnected I am to the work I do, the more I likely will not be able to deliver the necessary results.

In theory, there is one final authority that is critical to organizational success, but it takes years to build up. **This is that I have the right to appeal to my boss's boss when I am in chronic difficulty with my boss.** The key here is chronic difficulty. The rationale for this is first to reinforce trust in our leadership. Second, the boss's boss is the only one who holds my boss accountable for being a good leader or manager. There are mechanics to making this system work, but we have found that when our clients have implemented this authority, it changes the focus of the boss's boss. They now need to be more engaged in the work of their managerial leaders and check to see that they are caring for their people. This authority becomes a harbinger. Gradually a shift begins to occur. I know many human resources types who get upset and cry foul that the cats are watching the canaries. But in our experience, it is not true, especially in organizations where they make managerial leadership a profession. For too long we have not trusted management and have instead relied on human resources to be shop stewards to protect employees from big, bad management. It is time for managerial leaders to take back the night and build the organization the way it needs to be. It is time for professional managerial leadership.

Management Accountability

MANAGERIAL ACCOUNTABILITY FOR THE OUTPUT OF THE TEAM

The accountabilities don't stop there. I am also accountable to my manager for my management and leadership account-abilities as a manager. **First is that I am accountable to my manager for the output of my team.** This means that their success or failure is my success or problem. I can't blame my team, and in turn I have to assess their effectiveness, but they can't be held accountable for the team output. If they are responding to my direction, I wear any output issues. **The authority is that I need to be able to veto someone coming into my team. If I am accountable for the output, then I need to have a say in who comes into my team and initiate their removal from the team.** This is the work of managerial leaders and not human resources. It needs to rest with those directing the work. So the decision on whether someone is removed from my team should be approved by my boss, and in turn they should have a veto on someone I want to bring into my team.

MANAGERIAL ACCOUNTABILITY FOR THE BEHAVIOR OF THE TEAM

I also must be accountable to my boss for the behavior of my direct reports. For example, I am accountable to my boss that they behave safely and respect one another. It is not their responsibility; it is my accountability, and I need to be ready to step in to ensure their safety individually. I must be the only one to assign them work to accomplish this. We should have only one boss. For example, if my boss starts assigning work to my team on top of what I assign them, they are left with the problem of figuring out on which side their bread is buttered.

A critical premise of accountability is that I can have only one boss. The matrix organizations or dotted line organizational charts are really just manifestations of abrogating our roles as managerial leaders to define the work for our people. Just like the executives who felt it couldn't be done, organizations give up too fast and wonder why there is confusion among their people. The most important authority that a manager needs to have is to be the one who signs off on the performance evaluation and recommends consequences whether good or bad. This is the core of accountability, and when we take that away from our managers, they are left with lifeless consequence mechanisms. Too often, in order to curb responsibility, we take this away, giving it to a committee to adjudicate. What we have done is neutered our leaders. We have reinforced that we cannot trust our leaders. Putting objective roadblocks in their way has hampered their ability to hold people accountable and therefore hindered *our* success. The manager is held to account by their manager, and in turn their manager is held to account by their manager. It is a chain, and as soon as we break that chain because best practice says, then we have undermined our managers' ability to connect the people and the task.

MANAGERIAL ACCOUNTABILITY:
GROW THE CAPABILITY OF YOUR TEAM

As a leader, I am accountable to build a team of increasingly capable direct reports. This means that my boss holds me accountable to develop my people. There are a couple of facets to this. One is that the perfect candidate is not out there. If you have that unicorn, hang on to it. But the reality is that people have to grow and develop in their roles, and it is their boss's job to oversee this. If you want to win the war for talent, make this your credo. You will be an employer of choice. If you leave it to employees to develop themselves out of a sense of responsibility, then expect to see turnover. The other rationale is that you, as the leader, know what you expect of them, so only you can develop them. There is no magic training out there. You need to coach them and develop them yourself. If you follow this logic, then your manager is accountable to their boss to develop *you* as a managerial leader—suddenly it isn't your sense of responsibility to develop yourself.

MANAGERIAL ACCOUNTABILITY:
LEADING YOUR TEAM

The next accountability is to lead your team. Your leader needs to assess how you lead your team. Are you out in front or never seen and not engaged? In my experience, too many leaders leave it to their people and don't lead them. The phrase "I will tell you when you do something wrong" is not leading your people. To lead them, you need to be present and in the moment. In my experience, bosses sense when a leader is present or not. The trick is to not wait until you have all the data you need to trust your instincts. Too many times I have seen leaders wait until they have a solid court case, and by then the offending leader has done irreparable harm to the team. Trust your instincts and senses, because your manager is holding you accountable too. If there is smoke, there is fire, so get in and search it out, remembering, of course, that you are accountable for the working behaviors of your team. Better that you sort it out before your boss sorts you out.

MANAGERIAL ACCOUNTABILITY:
PRACTICE CONTINUOUS IMPROVEMENT

The final accountability is a management accountability, and that is to practice continuous improvement in your team. Managers need to practice continuous improvement and always look for opportunities to make things better. Best advice is a tool to help you make it an everyday occurrence in your team and not relegated to the anonymous suggestion box. **There is also leadership continuous improvement, which is spending time improving your people's capability.** This is a subset of building team accountability, but it highlights how you can create a learning organization. So a critical leadership accountability is to coach our people.

> By coaching, we get the performance we want.

By coaching, we get the performance we want. We create

learning organizations and continuously improve. Just as it is the employee's right to be coached, it is the accountability of the manager to coach their people. Coaching, and by extension feedback, is not a black art. You don't need a secret decoder ring. It is merely a conversation about performance to get a direct report from where they are to a more desired end state. It is not to be feared. That said, leaders need to be held accountable by their leaders to coach their people. It is a critical skill of the managerial leader and has to be treated as such. It is the enabler to organizational success, and managerial leaders need to do it regularly. It is closely related to consequences because coaching is the vessel by which good and bad consequences are meted out.

The Manager Once Removed

There is one final list of accountabilities and authorities, and those are of the manager once removed. The manager once removed is critical in the accountability management framework and key to organizational success. A manager once removed is a manager of managers. They are key because they are accountable to their manager to **hold their direct report managers accountable for being good managers.** This role ensures the translation of strategy and the adherence to the profession of managerial leadership. Here managers are held accountable to be good managers and to exercise managerial leadership. This starts at the director level and moves all the way to the CEO. Without this accountability, it is just about relying on managers to feel *obliged* to be good managers. I learned this **critical** lesson while training managers—that their manager needs to be involved and hold them accountable to behave differently. The accountabilities don't stop there. The manager once removed is the one who needs to ensure the development and succession in their broader team. We call this **the accountability to develop the talent pool of their direct reports.** They will delegate the act of development, but they are accountable to their manager to develop them and mentor them in the career paths.

> Clients of ours who have implemented this approach realize that this is where the real value lies.

Clients of ours who have implemented this approach realize that this is where the real value lies. No longer are you finding your replacement as so many gurus state, but rather the individual with the biggest purview is the one who is accountable to look at the talent and develop paths to grow them for the long run. This simple system ensures succession for the longer term, but it also does more. The combination of my manager coaching me in my day-to-day performance and having a manager once removed also focused on my career path makes this a great place to work where I am truly valued and not just a number. The final accountability is a management one. It is critical to the smooth functioning of the business, and this role is **accountable to their boss for defining the cross-functional relationships between their direct reports once removed.** This is where authority is defined. If my direct report once removed X needs service from another direct report once removed Y, I am accountable to define that relationship. There will be more on this later. But it is this role that enables work to flow across the organization, and it is this role starting at the CEO that laterally integrates the business. The manager once removed defines for their Team One what will be the interrelationships in the Team Twos to make the organization work. According to our clients, the time spent on this is the most valuable, and without time expended here, your strategy is at risk. Without this role and its accountabilities, the organizational pain will be incapacitating in the long run.

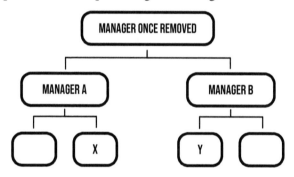

The integration of all these accountabilities and authorities is what enables organizational success. But the mind shift is equally important. We need to really understand what accountability means and how it helps. By that token, we can't ignore responsibility because it ensures commitment. It is really a matter of sequence. By building accountability and authority first, you can then expect responsibility. But for the managerial leader, it is clear that there is no place for them to hide because, in the well-working organization, the managers and leaders of leaders are professional and are making sure first and foremost that the accountability management system is working.

FOR MANAGERS OF MANAGERS:
THE TABLE OF ACCOUNTABILITY AND AUTHORITY

Accountability (The Expectation)	Authority (The Legitimated Power)
As Employees	
Commit to do the work given by my manager.	Be clear on work and resources. Be safe physically.
Work at the level expected of me.	Be coached by someone more capable than me.
Give my manager my best advice.	Be safe physically, psychologically, and socially.
Stay within the values.	Appeal to my boss's boss when in chronic difficulty with my manager.
As Managers	
Manage outputs of the team.	Veto someone coming into the team. Initiate removal from the team.
Manage behaviors of the team.	Be the only one to assign work to team members.
Build a team of increasingly capable direct reports.	Be coached by someone more capable than me.
Lead the team.	Be the only one to assign work to team members.
Practice continuous improvement.	Be safe physically, psychologically, and socially.
Coach your people.	Be coached by someone more capable than me.
Accountabilities as Managers Once Removed	
Hold direct report managers accountable for being good managers.	
Develop the talent pool.	
Define the cross-functional role relationships.	

Milestone #3: Accountability

You have reached a very important milestone on your journey. Take the time to pause, rest, and refresh by really thinking about accountability, responsibility, and authority. It is at the core of organizational pain, and if you take the time here to reflect, you will start to remove the pain I discussed in chapter 2. You will progress toward the profession of managerial leadership and set the pathway to be that great manager of managers. In the next chapter, we will discuss core management skills to supercharge your journey to accountability and authority.

Is your organization based on accountability, or does it rely on responsibility to be successful?

What are the implications of this?

What do you need to do?

How effective are you at managing the spectrum of consequence? Where do you focus +/-?

Where does that come from?

Where will you focus your energy?

How effective are your managers at managing the spectrum of consequence? Where are they focused +/-?

Why?

What do you need to do to change this?

How committed are your managers to their work as managers?

How do you know?

Who needs encouragement and how?

What is the quality of the best advice you are getting?

Are you giving best advice?

If not, why not?

Are your managers getting best advice?

How do you know?

If not, why not?

Is the emphasis of your managers on the output or the behaviors?

What needs to change?

How will you change it?

Are your managers leading their teams?

How do you know?

What will you do?

Are your managers coaching and growing their people?

How do you know?

What will you do?

How well are you holding your direct report managers accountable for being good managers?

How do you know?

What do you need to do?

How well have you developed the talent pool?

Do you have successors for your direct report managers?

What will you do about it?

Have you defined the cross-functional role relationships?

What are the implications of not doing it?

What will you do about it?

CHAPTER 4

THE ENGAGED MANAGER: A MANAGER OF MANAGERS' DAY IN THE LIFE

If your managers are not engaged, you can never expect your employees to be.

One of my clients had a complex business that required extensive cross-functional work and relied on different departments with various capabilities to work together in harmony. The problem was that they could not. They worked at odds with one another. There was infighting between teams and inside teams, and everyone was always trying to second-guess each other. In an attempt to find a solution, I reached back to my experience to consider the best models of cross-functional teams. I went back to my army experiences with what is known as the combat team. A combat team is an organization that works with many different skills and expertise to achieve a common mission. Usually more than two hundred people make up a combat team. They are multidisciplinary, with engineers, infantry (foot soldiers), armored (tanks), and artillery (big guns). When they work together, there is a mutual trust among all and a camaraderie of a common mission, even though everyone has different skills. It has the flexibility to adjust to who commands it based on predetermined and established standards. Even the most junior of leaders can command what seniors do based on the circumstance. The tactical successes of operations in Afghanistan and Iraq were the result of this interdisciplinary flexibility. What makes it work is good management. With this model, we set about defining what needed to be done to make this team effective, and it was all about management skills.

The Essence of Great Teams Lies in Great Management

With this in mind, how do we create these great teams for our organization? It is through management, and that comes by ensuring that we have engaged managers. We can't expect that they feel responsible to be engaged; rather, we need to hold them accountable. We need to encourage them through positive consequences but also make sure they are aware of what they need to do. Recognition is a form of positive consequence, and people need it. They need to know if they are on track. For a team to be effective, it needs to have clarity of purpose and an alignment of common work for the common weal. This requires sizeable yet worthwhile time spent getting all things organized. It is through management that the strategy is translated into clear work. However, the starting point is clear work and work expectations to deliver the strategy. Management creates a sustainable system by clearly defining the work. What in turn sustains that are solid management practices, the most important being managing managers.

The Science of Management

There is a science to management, and that science comes from understanding the nature of work and the human condition at work. Far too often we are slipshod in how we design work. Structure is the system of accountabilities within organizations. The purpose of structure is to implement the strategy, and it consists of roles, role relationships, and processes. Good structure makes managing easier. In turn good structure facilitates teamwork and trust. Since structure is the *foundation* of delivering strategy, this is the management work of managerial leadership. To be clear, for this structure to work, it cannot be assigned to human resources. Human resources can be the technical experts who advise and potentially provide oversight and assistance to the CEO, but this is the work of managers. **The masters of this have to be the managers of managers.** It is their role to design the work.

I find with a lot of our clients that they design work based upon incumbency. The work is planned solely based upon the capability of the incumbent of the role. This we define as strategy from structure. If an organization is designed based purely upon the employees' current capabilities, then it is going to struggle to be able to deliver its strategy. It will be forever searching for perfect candidates, which is a fool's errand. Instead, what is required is a thorough understanding of the strategy and then devising the necessary structure to deliver it. This is key to accountability: clarity of what the work is. As we saw earlier, the **first authority** of employees is to be clear on their work and resources. We have done two types of experiments to prove that this is a reality. In workshops we have asked people to define what they are accountable for. We have found that people are good at describing the activities, but they stumble on what that end state is to represent. Essentially, we are good at defining what we do but not what we are to deliver. The **second authority** is seen (or not seen) when we ask managers to define the work of their direct reports, and 30 percent feel they need to ask their direct reports before committing. If you find your organization in this position, it is driven by a sense of responsibility, and your managers are absent. But if the manager is absent, it isn't that manager's issue (yet); instead, it is the fault of the manager of that manager. This is a paradigm shift that gets to the heart of accountability.

> If an organization is designed based purely upon the employees' current capabilities, then it is going to struggle to be able to deliver its strategy.

Understanding Organizational Structure: The Science

What does a manager of managers need to know and understand in order to create that engaged manager? First, they need to increase their professional understanding of organizational structure. Structure defines how people work. It cannot be guesswork. Structure needs to be rooted in science and application. The best framework we have found to understand the nature of the human condition in organizations is the stratified systems theory.[3] In essence, this theory defines the nature of the various levels of work in organizations. The levels represent levels of complexity and capability that are required for an organization to work. Each of these levels performs certain functions. The farther up you go, the more complex the work becomes, and it requires a different capability. Once you have defined the work and its complexity, you can match the right person for the role. You don't want to put someone into a more complex role than they can handle because that would add too much stress to the individual and be unfair. By the same token, you don't want to put someone into a role below their capability because they will be bored and leave. You need to get it just right, with enough stress to create the tension to pull them forward—but not too much. We call this the Goldilocks principle. The idea is to get it just right, not too big and not too small. When managers don't get it right, it becomes no fun for the employee. You want to create that

---

3   Elliott Jaques, *Requisite Organization* (London, Gower, 1979).

great place to work where someone is challenged, not bored and not overwhelmed. This is the first step to creating that great place to work.

SOME EXAMPLES OF LEVELS

To give you a sense of these levels, most organizations are no more than five levels of complexity from the front line to the president/CEO.

A six-level organization will have two or more business units, and a seven-level organization is a multinational with many different businesses. In the military, the five-level organization is the equivalent of a division and a six-level organization is a corps.

In a consulting meeting with the CEO of a mid-tier financial institution, I made it clear that based on his strategy, his structure needed to be a five-level organization. He responded, "That would be way too many levels and would reduce my flexibility." I already had a sense that his structure was likely not that flexible and asked to see his organizational chart. When he and I pored over the chart, it was clear that there were eight levels.

Without understanding levels and having a structure based on incumbency, most organizations range from eight to ten levels for what should be five. We get managers reporting to senior managers and directors reporting to associate vice presidents and so on. The culprit for this is incumbency. We want to recognize not by personal connection but by titles.

As Machiavelli said, "It is not titles that honor men, but men that honor titles."

We also add layers and levels when the people we have are not working at the level necessary. This is further exacerbated if the manager doesn't work at their appropriate level, preferring instead to work a level below, causing your structure to become even more messed up.

Compression and Gaps

The levels in stratified systems theory are not arbitrary. They are based on human capability and what is required for the work. When we don't understand these levels, we create too many levels, and we create compression when there are too many levels. Compression's hallmarks are bureaucracy and micromanagement as people try to add value (out of a sense of responsibility). In other cases, we arbitrarily remove levels, and this in turn creates gaps. The hallmarks of gaps are confusion and discontinuity in the organization. All of these cost the organization wasted time, which equals wasted money. Things get worse when you add titles and title inflation, which brings about even more confusion and misunderstanding. People place a value on titles. Somehow they signify power, but in a good structure, it is the work interrelationship that is important, not someone's title. Structure needs principles and foundations before you add people to the mix. Sometimes you have to design outside the science, but as long as you have the foundation, then you can make decisions with a full understanding of the impact and you are able to mitigate any potential ill effects. The manager of managers performs a critical role because they plan the structure not only of the next level but also one level farther down. This is because the manager defines the work of their direct reports and gives their direct reports the resources to fulfill their role. In this way the director level (the first level of managers of managers) defines the structure for the front line. This is after their manager, the vice president, has defined the work of their directors and given them their managers as resources. As you can see, this is why it is important for the manager of managers to be a professional manager and to understand structure.

LEVEL X+2	
LEVEL X+1	MANAGER
LEVEL X	?
LEVEL X-1	DIRECT REPORT

Gaps

LEVEL X+2	
LEVEL X+1	
LEVEL X	MANAGER
	DIRECT REPORT
LEVEL X-1	

Compression

Lateral Functions

In our experience, the levels are what most organizations don't get. They do understand the lateral functions. But we have found that often we need to provide perspective here as well. There are five lateral functions for organizations to structure themselves around, and often there is a combination of these. They are typically functional, geographic, customer, technology, and process. For example, a sales function may have a geographic structure at one level and then a technology or customer delineation within that geography. The important part for managers of managers to remember is that the structure needs to be clear and easy for everyone to navigate. Navigation is the part that organizations fail at. By our calculations, almost 75 percent of work occurs laterally across organizations.[4] For example, the value chain for retail of plan, buy, move, and sell often requires three functions to work laterally together for success.

---

4   Nick Forrest, *How Dare You Manage?: Seven Principles to Close the CEO Skill Gap,* Toronto, ON, BPS Books, 2013.

In incumbency-based structures, we know who to go to in order to get things done until there is a change. New hires often struggle for months to find that right person to pass work off to or get help from. What happens is that we have to rely on our relationships just to get the work done. By having a clear, navigable structure, we can enable people and not have to rely on the old I-know-a-guy-who-can-set-you-up construct; I've referred to this as the backroom drug deal. In addition to not finding someone to assist you, the real problem with this loose approach to working is that it laterally damages trust.

In a simple scenario, when I rely on my relationship to get help, I can usually get my friend to help me. In a simple case of providing service, my friend agrees, but as time goes on, my friend gets overloaded with work. When I come to collect my service, I find that it isn't there. Now my work is in jeopardy, and I can no longer trust my friend and the spiral begins. The real issue is that the provided service needs to be defined, and my coworker needs to be held to account by his manager to provide it. That way it isn't about the relationship; it is just about the work. This is back to the authority I need for me to get service, and it must be overseen and exercised by management. This can look simple, but when acrimony flares up, trust is damaged and we don't deliver the strategy.

We spend time helping our clients to work through the interrelationships of roles because it is there that issues within the organization get resolved. The discipline to clarify who has the hammer to get service, who can tell others when they need to stop doing what they are doing, and who has the authority to call meetings are the authorities. Too often the tyranny of do sets in while the organization tilts at another windmill instead of cleaning up what needs fixing. It requires discipline and sticking to it instead of charging at the windmills. To clean up relationships in reality is like the EDS commercial of building an aircraft while in flight. It requires managers to maintain the focus and remove the roadblocks while keeping the plane flying.

Anaklesis: The Universal Challenge

Where to put real people into the structure brings us to the universal issue: It needs to be addressed, and we must strive to reduce tensions in relationships. The single greatest barrier to effective management, change, and collaboration is what we term *anaklesis*: the very human, ingrained need we all have to rely (or lean) upon beliefs or individuals.

Humans do not resist change itself, nor do we avoid hard truths for the truth they contain. Rather, we resist the pain of losing those things upon which we depend. We lean on habits, beliefs, and relationships as a form of control over our lives, and the fear of losing those is a barrier to personal and organizational growth. Sigmund Freud first identified anaklesis in the early twentieth century. It is rooted in the nature of analytic depression. Psychologists continued research on the topic through the midcentury, when it was picked up by the management writer Jerry Harvey and then later Forrest's team member, Dr. Herb Koplowitz.

Anaklesis is like a dance: It occurs whenever two or more people come together with the natural, primary purpose of looking good and not stepping on each other's toes. Rather than discussing tough issues, they begin the dance; the desire to be liked, avoid hurting anyone's feelings, and be seen as agreeable takes precedence. When I went to my friend to ask for service, I would have had to overcome my fear of damaging the relationship by asking for something. In turn he would likely have suffered from anaklesis, and so as not to endanger the relationship, he didn't tell me he couldn't deliver. Now we are left with me not trusting him, and because of my anaklesis, I have not told him this, and so the conflict goes underground and damages the organization. **Anaklesis is rampant in today's organizations, where being nice is overemphasized and strong relationships are valued over effective relationships.**

Anaklesis is very real. For an organization to operate in this environment, it is necessary to remove the potential of anaklesis by making the work just about work. Employees should not have to screw up their courage to work with one another. There are enough stresses already, so why make it harder for them? If someone is to provide a service, they need to be held accountable to do so, just as the employee who is asking for it needs to be held accountable to ask for it as part of their job. Anaklesis leads to dysfunction, and its most profound impact is on managerial leadership. Many managers will avoid having tough conversations to build trust and friendly relationships, when in fact it has the opposite effect. It is anaklesis that gets in the way of them having the necessary conversations as part of their work. In turn anaklesis gets in the way of employees having open and honest dialogue to advise their boss. In my career, I wished I could replay the scenario so that employees/soldiers could have told me I was wearing no clothes. Instead, there I went, as oblivious as the

> Anaklesis leads to dysfunction, and its most profound impact is on managerial leadership.

emperor. Anaklesis kept them from telling me the truth, and way too often I softened the blow of a necessary conversation only to water down the effect and create confusion. This is why best advice is an accountability rather than a responsibility. Its purpose is to remove anaklesis. My job as managerial leader is not about me; it is about the role I perform. All the literature on management and leadership overlooks the critical roles that managers of managers perform. They keep the organization going in one direction. They define the structure and ensure that the ethics and integrity of the organization are maintained. But most importantly, they reduce anaklesis and help their direct report managers overcome their own anaklesis.

Where anaklesis also rears its head is in our reluctance to change. We lean on our old ways of doing things and on our old beliefs. Anaklesis makes me reluctant to give up what I lean on and instead prefer what I already know and have experienced. It isn't that I am change resistant and that this is some kind of label that I carry like a scarlet letter. Rather, it is that I am leaning on those old ways.

If you wonder how this takes shape in reality, look at the new employee. What do they talk about for the first eighteen months? They talk of what it was like in their old place. Not because they like it better but because they are leaning on that experience to feel whole in the new environment.

It is hard for me to overcome my anaklesis, and that is where my manager comes in. My main need is to see the new way and not succumb to my anaklesis, or worse, to be set by the side of the road while the organization goes on without me.

Managers suffer from both forms of anaklesis. It is the work of managers of managers to help them overcome their fear of damaging relationships or their reticence to change. The work of managers of managers is to ensure that they have engaged managers. An engaged manager understands how to utilize the structure in a disciplined way and apply it to the people. The connection of people and structure is essential. Structure comes alive when it has the right people in those roles. The roles are right because they are founded on the strategy, but how do you make sure you have the right people in the roles? It is all about complexity. Just as levels were defined by complexity, so is our capability. Our ability to handle complexity is our governor.

Human Capability

Human capability is made up of four things: attitude and motivation, the ability to behave reasonably, skills and knowledge, and cognitive capacity. Regarding the first, attitude and motivation, do your people truly value the work they are doing? Have they found new outlets for their energy and passion? There are many things we don't like in our work, but generally we value our work and are willing to put discretionary effort into it.

The second, the ability to behave reasonably, requires a certain amount of judgment and discretion to identify. If faced with the tensions and stresses of daily work, can I generally behave reasonably? If I cannot, do I resort to substance abuse or become abusive to others?

The third is the most common in assessing human capability, and that is do we have the skills and knowledge and experience for our role? It is either what we are born with or develop through experience, coaching, or training. Beware that while this is the easiest of the four to assess, it can be misleading. Interestingly enough, unless you were in the public health realm, no one had the skills and knowledge for COVID-19, so everyone was flying blind. We have placed inordinate emphasis on skills, knowledge, and experience, and there are challenges there beyond the fact that I may not have had the experience. If my experience was fundamentally different elsewhere, it may have no value now. There is a lesson here: you shouldn't put all your emphasis on skills and knowledge because, if you do, you will have people who are brilliant in the day-to-day, but they may not be able to adapt when change comes along.

The final element of human capability is the governor because it defines whether we can use our skills and knowledge and apply them in new circumstances. It is the secret sauce that, when the individual has this and the other three, they can take off. It is the ability to handle the complexity of the role they are in. Can they think through the work? Can they find ways to solve issues? It is the governor on their capability. Because if they don't have it, they will ultimately be unsuccessful. In the case of COVID-19, we had to rely on people's cognitive capacity to develop solutions and not just on their skills and knowledge.

FOUR ELEMENTS

As a workplace example, we have all seen the person who is doing a brilliant job, and we promote them. Then things start to slide, so we get coaching or training to help them. But as time goes on, they become more withdrawn and start to arrive late for work and are disengaged. Eventually we have to let them go. The issue now feels like attitude and motivation. The real issue was that they were promoted beyond their cognitive capacity, and they could not handle the complexity. This is often known as the Peter principle. The converse is true as well. For years, the individual who has done the same job seems a bit quirky, always trying new ways of doing things, and just doesn't fit in. Eventually they leave independently, finding more challenging work or a better manager. In an accountability framework, the issue was not theirs but ours as the leader. We had thrown them into the Sahara or a tiny sandbox. Again, this is the leader's fault. These levels of cognitive capacity are like the surface of water. It is hard to keep a beach ball below the surface and hard to pull up a boulder. The trick is the Goldilocks principle. Or in other words, give them the role that is just right. In reality, this cognitive capacity becomes their potential. Their potential in the current role with all the other elements right also defines their future potential.

Application of Human Capability to Work

Now let's discuss human capability through the lens of management. First off, your managers need to value the work of management. That may seem simple, but trust me, there are many who don't. Managers have to overcome these issues to be successful. They can't know it innately. They need to be coached by their boss to either get onto the management bus or find another role. If you find that there are issues of managers not behaving reasonably, this is not something the average manager of managers is equipped to deal with. In my experience with posttraumatic stress disorder, this is the work of experts. You need to identify it and assist them in getting the help they need. Human resources can help you here, but this is a path for them to deal with using the appropriate resources. When it comes to skills, knowledge, and experience, the skillful and professional manager of managers can diagnose the issues. If it is a technical issue, coaching and training may be needed. However, remember that their work is to manage the technical. Of course, it is valuable to understand it, but they need not be experts. Too often managers feel anaclitic because they have no skills to lean on. As a result, they lay back or avoid the work rather than engaging their team.

You need to be alert to this form of imposter syndrome, where they feel they just don't have the skills to engage. It can be very damaging, just as overconfidence and a desire to prove they have the skills can also be damaging. These are two sides of the same coin and need to be addressed by clarifying what the work really is. The manager of managers must spend their time focused on the managerial leadership skills of their direct reports, for this is their *real* work. All our efforts need to be about managerial leadership. It can be coached and taught, and who better to do it than their boss.

Cognitive Capacity and Management

To begin with, employees prefer to be led by people who have a greater degree of cognitive capacity than themselves. In fact, they *must* have greater cognitive capacity, otherwise the manager adds no value to their work. Managers add value in three ways regardless of their technocratic know-how. If your managers practice these three things, they will add value to their direct reports, and it comes from their cognitive capacity.

* The first is that they add context. They get context from their manager, and by virtue of their cognitive capacity, they can explain why and how the work fits together.

✳ The second is that they are the ones who know what the end state for the work needs to be. They know how it fits into the strategy and what is expected in the end with the culmination of Team Two's work.

✳ Finally, they know where to get the resources because they sit at a different level and they have a bigger picture.

The manager of managers adds real value because they are the ones who know what is expected of their direct report managers, and this is why the manager of managers needs to be intimately involved in talent planning and development. Only the manager of managers can tell if someone might have the cognitive capacity for the next level. The manager is in the role and cannot necessarily assess whether their people have the potential for the next level. If their direct reports could, then they would already be at the next level. Your direct report managers will have a sense that they are able to handle more complex work, but the manager of managers is the final arbiter. The manager of managers ensures the integration of the people with the needs of the work.

Consistent Management

Managers of managers ensure a consistent management approach across all their managers. The approach needs to be universal and timeless, bypassing the whims of the organizational development community and flavors of the month and going to the very heart of what it means to be a manager.

The manager of managers establishes the standards for all their managers and ensures a common framework for those managers.

Leadership or management skills training often is scattershot and is not aligned to business outcomes. What is necessary is a common framework that is comprehensive and not focused on just one skill set as identified by engagement or employee pulse surveys. In my experience, civilian management training does not teach these. They tend to be very singular in their method, and they don't really develop a universal approach to management. A classic example is the drive to develop coaching skills. Pretty soon all the managers are having their training passports updated with a coaching skills

> **Leadership or management skills training often is scattershot and is not aligned to business outcomes.**

training program. The problem is that the training, while valuable, is out of context. It is out of context to the accountabilities addressed in chapter 3 and often doesn't last because we don't hold the managers accountable to do it. To create the change you need, you must have a consistent universal set of skills and the framework of accountability exercised by managers of managers to ensure that the learning is implemented. Too often the managers of managers leave this work to the trainers, not realizing that their work is to establish these frameworks and to hold their managers accountable to apply them.

There are four key practices that managers of managers need to ensure that their managers are proficient at and are using regularly: aligning, building, connecting, and delegating the ABCDs of management.

Aligning Your Teams and People

The first of the practices, aligning, is about getting the team and your direct reports aligned to the tasks at hand. It is about lateral integration. It clarifies why direct reports are doing the work they are doing, and it is about the manager being aligned with their manager's goals and objectives. This is known as the cascade of leadership influence, and it ensures a seamless plan of action for the entire organization based on the objectives from the very top of the organization. It involves clarity for the manager on what their manager wants

> Managers of managers can ensure alignment by demonstrating and discussing with their direct reports both context and insight into how their work fits into the bigger picture.

and what their manager once removed wants. It requires a manager to use their judgment and discretion to make plans and align the team based on their managers' plans. It is about open dialogue to explain why and to get input on how it could be different.

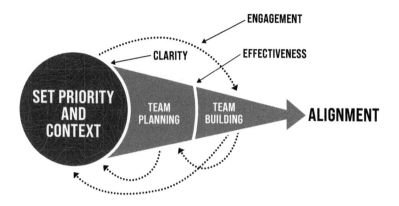

Alignment relies on three main activities that a manager must do, which are setting context, planning the work for the team, and then building the team. One of the skills that we find missing the most is setting context. Too many times managers brush over this important step, which leads to confusion, mistrust, and disenchantment in their teams. Without context, people are free to make up all sorts of stories about why things are happening, and the conspiracy theories abound. Managers of managers can ensure alignment by demonstrating and discussing with their direct reports both context and insight into how their work fits into the bigger picture. In the army there is an old trick. The senior officer walks around and asks the troops if they are clear on context and what the plan is. Woe betide the officer whose soldiers don't know. There is a huge payoff if they know the context and the plan, as they are more engaged and therefore you get better best advice.

It is the work of the manager of managers to make sure that their managers are aligning their teams.

Building Your Teams

The next practice, building, is about creating a team of the manager's choosing. It is the active selection process to create the best possible team. But it doesn't stop there. It is about integrating the new member to the team and integrating the team to the new member. Too often this critical step is overlooked, and it creates animosity in the team and a sense of dejection in the new member. It is about change, and ongoing change, to make sure that the team is finely honed. This focus of change and desire to change is critical for a manager. Building is about making the tough decisions of removing people from the team if they detract from the goal. Removing someone from the team enforces the team because the team recognizes that that member was not a good fit for the role and might be better suited to an area where they can be successful. It is a clear case of using judgment and discretion to make tough decisions for the betterment of the team and the individual. Building a level of comfort for change with direct reports is about guiding them and giving them a sense that they can go farther and faster. This is the essence of continuous improvement.

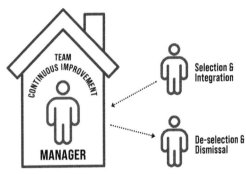

It is the manager's role to build each member of the team to actively work to improve at all levels in their work. Managers of managers need to take an active interest in selecting their direct reports once removed because this is the farm team of succession. They also need to make sure that the integration goes well and that their managers lead it. On the point of continuous improvement, it is through management that we exercise continuous improvement. Programs and systems are all good to assist them, but it needs to be driven by managers; otherwise, you will merely have people feeling responsible. Where our clients have implemented this, they have defined roles to assist management, and they also have authority clearly delineated, but it is still the managers of managers who ensure continuous improvement.

Connecting the People to the Work

The connecting practice is simply connecting with direct reports to get the output that the manager needs and to help direct reports achieve the goals set for them. It is the mechanism by which a manager engages direct reports and sets them on the path to effectiveness. It is about helping and encouraging direct reports rather than leaving them to flounder. It is important to do this in conjunction with building because it not only provides the mechanisms for assessment of individuals, which in turn can help in deselection and dismissal deliberations, but also can encourage continuous improvement. Connecting is when the manager becomes real to their direct reports. Connecting is always done in dialogue to engage two-way communication. This requires trust to be effective.

> Someone who is not real, honest, forthright, and trustworthy will not be able to engage direct reports.

Someone who is not real, honest, forthright, and trustworthy will not be able to engage direct reports. Finally, it requires the use of judgment and discretion on the manager's part to step up and make assessments of the individual. Connecting includes monitoring the work, coaching, and assessing effectiveness.

On this last piece, the manager of managers has an important role to play. There has been a perception that performance evaluation is not a valuable exercise for too long. I argue that it is not the process that lacks value; it is the fact that managers have not been held to account to make it valuable. It has been left to a once-a-year slugfest with a variety of processes that have merely watered down the manager's input. To be clear, it is the manager's job to always be assessing performance. It is their role and a critical authority that they have. They must assess, and watering it down with the employee's view merely denigrates the importance. It is done in dialogue, which means in conjunction. It isn't done *to* the employee. The employee should value it because their manager should be more capable than them. If not, then the manager of the manager should replace that manager with the direct report.

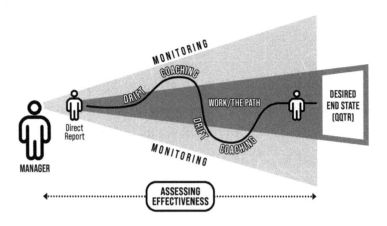

Delegating Work

Probably one of the most essential and least effectively employed practices is delegating. It is important to remember that delegating is a gift that enables others to use their creativity and their capability. It is the foundation of empowerment because it gives others their work. Good delegation releases the capability of the organization and is a skill that also encompasses

> Good delegation releases the capability of the organization and is a skill that also encompasses aligning and connecting.

aligning and connecting. It requires alignment to launch the delegating, and it needs monitoring, coaching, and assessing effectiveness to deliver the necessary results.

Many managers feel that they have adequately delegated, yet they cannot understand why their direct reports did not give the results they wanted. Often a manager's last question is,

"Did I not make it clear what I wanted?" The reasons for this are numerous, but most revolve around the discomfort about telling someone to do something on the one hand and being too overbearing on the other. Again, judgment and discretion are necessary to deal with this. A manager must be comfortable putting forward both objective views and subjective opinions.

Delegating is the process used to get the work done. It is based on the need to get things done through the work of others. Delegation requires trust and dialogue as much as any of the other practices. It also needs to include alignment. Delegating must be aligned to the organization's needs, and direct reports must be clear on the context for the delegation to provide their best advice. In cases where their discretion is to be used, they also need to know the big picture. While this is the last practice discussed, it is the essence of accountability. As such, managers of managers need to spend time ensuring that the system is in place and is working. Instead of SMART goals in accountability, we advocate using QQTR for setting clearly smart goals.

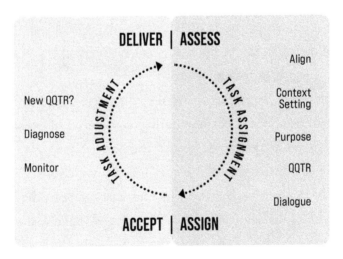

Effectively delegating tasks to direct reports is a challenge for managers at any level. Without clearly defining a task, the work can be completed below or above expectation. In both instances, resources are ineffectively used. The model we recommend is for managers to define QQTR. Rather than the popular SMART goals, QQTR clearly defines an end state. The manager sets context as to the why we discussed earlier, then defines the quantity, the quality, the time when it needs to be completed, and what resources they have to assist them. The

> **Effectively delegating tasks to direct reports is a challenge for managers at any level.**

quantity defines how many things need to be produced. It is objective and quantifiable. The quality defines the standard and how it will be perceived and is subjective in many cases. The time projects to a future intended time, and resources can be anything to help. The advantage of QQTR is that you merely adjust the parameters along the way if the situation changes. But it is the manager's work to define it in dialogue and adjust it. That way, the QQTR is always achieved and there are no surprises.

Earlier I discussed the combat team. The combat team is successful because everyone knows their role and can adapt to changing circumstances. It has the right people in the roles to be able to drive success, and it has a common set of practices, or SOPs (standard operating procedures). But all of these things must also be done by careful management and by the critical role of the manager of managers. This enables mission success and ultimately strategy success.

You can create great places to work by ensuring that you have engaged managers. Understanding the importance of well-thought-out structure releases the capability of the organization. Being mindful of anaklesis and its implications will help to keep your managers on track, and following a common set of management practices will ensure your success. As the manager of managers, your role is to ensure the discipline to create that great place to work. It is easy to do; you just need to stick to it.

> You can create great places to work by ensuring that you have engaged managers.

The Management Practices	
Aligning	Setting context
	Team planning
	Team building
Building	Selecting and integrating talent
	Deselecting and dismissing
	Practicing continuous improvement
Connecting	Monitoring
	Coaching
	Assessing effectiveness
Delegating	Assigning tasks
	Adjusting tasks

Milestone #4: The Engaged Manager

Here you are at your fourth milestone. This chapter aims to set up the systems to enable decision-making and work to happen freely. There is a lot of work to be done here, so take the time at this milestone to reflect on where you and the organization are on this part of the journey. Will you need to circle back and revisit in time? What needs to be done to engage your managers? In the next chapter, we'll discuss the leadership ethos that will propel you and your leaders forward.

How many reporting levels are there in your organization?

Is the work clearly delineated between roles?

What do you need to do?

How clear is the workflow across functions?

How well do you support across functions?

What will you do about it?

Do your leaders suffer from anaklesis?

What needs to be done?

Are you anaclitic with them?

Consider any direct reports you may have challenges with. Is it a matter of skills and knowledge, not valuing the work, not being able to behave reasonably, or a lack of cognitive capacity?

How do you know?

What will you do?

How clear are your people on priority and context?

Why is it clear or not clear?

How can you improve this?

How clear are your people on your expectations?

How do you know?

How well are they cascading it?

How robust are your work planning systems?

How effective are your managers at planning?

What do you need to do?

How well do you integrate new team members?

How well do your managers integrate new members?

What are your selection success rates?

How quickly do you deal with issues where employees are not able to do the work?

How successful are you at reintegrating them elsewhere?

What needs to be done about this?

Do you have a culture of continuous improvement?

What is your attitude toward mistakes?

How do you learn from mistakes or successes?

How effective are you at monitoring the effectiveness of your managers?

How well do your managers monitor their people?

What will you do about it?

How much of your work is coaching your managers to be good managers?

How effective are your managers at coaching?

What will you do about it?

How much of your meetings and one-on-one discussions are about management and leadership issues?

Why is that?

What do you need to do about it?

How good are you at assessing effectiveness?

How good are your managers at assessing effectiveness?

What will you do about it?

How clear are your task assignments?

How clear are your manager's task assignments?

What will you do about it?

How well do you adapt tasks as circumstances change?

How well do your managers adapt as circumstances change?

How well do they keep you informed of changing situations?

CHAPTER 5

THE ENLIGHTENED LEADER: HOW TO LEAD PEOPLE

Without purpose we are destined to be buffeted by life never knowing why.

The year 2020 was an interesting time. Whether it was the impact on an individual's mental health or our inability to come together in groups, it profoundly affected people, their beliefs, and their sense of self.

The economic impact on individuals was massive as well. It had and will have a considerable effect, whether it was the fired, the furloughed, or the failed business. The vaporized assets from the market changes or even the turbulence as markets bounced around added to economic woes. In turn these financial and health woes added more powder to the fire of injustice.

We have reached a common denominator. In those days, we were all black and indigenous, and we cannot allow these injustices to go by with impunity. If nothing else, 2020 has taught us a new respect for the individual. That respect came when you saved lives by sending workers home and when you set up health and safety measures as they came back. For a time, we set aside profit for humanity. You cannot get out of your current circumstance until you learn what you *need* to learn about it. I believe that this new respect for humanity is that learning.

Enlightened Leadership

The previous paragraphs were written for a weekly management missive that I sent to my clients during the pandemic. They were written at the end of 2020, with a new day dawning in 2021, or so one thought at the time. What I believe was dawning was a realization of the importance of leadership. I refer to this as enlightened leadership. Like its earlier namesake, it came out of the Dark Ages of leadership. Those were the ages of the art of the deal and the Jack Welch management school books that defined the nature of capitalism at the expense of the people. It was a new age of the dark satanic mill. We lived in an age that valued only the all-elusive dollar. Where the Wall Street Gordon Gekkos of the world saw that "greed for lack of a better word was good," COVID-19 taught us that didn't work.

Enlightened from its Latin roots is *illustratum*, which means to "illustrate or serve as an example." The pandemic gave us an example and one to live by. I believe we saw a new age of understanding of the value of our people. That said, many didn't, and they were shamed into caring. They were shamed into it because while they may have valued task over people, they realized their own natural humanity as they, too, were faced with the very real physical and mental dangers of the virus.

ENLIGHTENED LEADERSHIP DEFINED

To be an enlightened leader is nothing new, but we can resurrect its precepts and live by them as an example. I am not the first to use this title, but I believe it is an important part of the future of work. It is about the nature of the sacred relationship between the leader and the individual. The leaders who are good at this will successfully keep their people. Those who don't recognize the change will not meet with the same success.

My definition of enlightened leadership is different from others. To be an enlightened leader, we need to practice three things: authentic, servant, and transformational leadership. For authentic leadership, we must have a heightened sense of self-awareness and be real to our core. Servant leadership cares for those who work for you and removes the interferences to their potential. Finally, transformational leadership is about continuously improving and transforming your team and organization.

While enlightened leadership is an important sense of responsibility, our leaders need to be held accountable to practice it. It is hard work to be an enlightened leader. It is easy to declare that this is really important, and it's easy to say, "Do the right thing"—until it becomes difficult. As we say in leadership development, it is easy to take a stand when there is no wind, but once the gales hit, that is different.

The tyranny of do is one such thing that gets in the way of being an enlightened leader. With our heads down, we forget the people for the spreadsheet. The tension of task makes it hard as well. So we are back to why the leader of leaders becomes such a critical player. My boss is the one who can help me overcome the tyranny of do and become the leader the organization needs. In our experience, junior leaders are the ones who have the least attachment to leadership traits. They have come up through organizations and then suddenly find themselves thrust into leadership roles for which they may have little interest, and they also may not truly value working with people. What I believe has exacerbated this situation is that, with the advent of COVID-19 and going forward, they find themselves all alone working from home.

We also see that another gap in leadership is usually at the mid-level, where the mid-level leaders don't know how to lead the leaders. As a result, for an enlightened leadership to grow in organizations, leaders had to rely on an individual leader's sense of personal feeling of obligation or their own internal compass regarding a sense of responsibility. The sudden forced distribution of workforces challenges the old ways and enforces that sense of responsibility, which by indications impact mid-level managers the most. COVID-19 made a whole new group of leaders face the challenge of leading distributed workforces, something they had never had to do before. Our research showed that employees relished the new-found freedom, but mid-level leaders felt they had lost touch. The leader needs their leader at whatever level they are to help them on their path, to overcome their fears and create the new realm of leadership.

The pandemic exacerbated the problem. In talking with various CEOs, I found that they had done a great job of connecting and holding their businesses together, exercising their leadership by engaging with employees in Zoom rooms or Teams sessions. The unintended consequence of this great work is that we may have left no role for *their* junior leaders. As I discussed earlier, the unintentional consequences of CEOs and executives engaging with the people are removing the role for the real leaders who are operating farther down the hierarchy.

Authentic Leadership

To understand the role of leaders of leaders in creating enlightened leaders, it is necessary to understand what makes up the three elements of enlightened leadership. The first element of enlightened leadership is authentic leadership. We define this as the leader being themselves. Having taken the time for introspection, an authentic leader has a heightened sense of self-awareness. They have pondered what makes them do what they do. That may seem odd, but too often we behave in a way to feed an unknown set of desires that have been programmed into us, either by DNA or experience. (In my experience, when someone tells me they are self-aware, they usually are not.) This awareness enables us to do the following:

* Understand our strengths and limitations.

* Understand our goals and objectives in life.

* Have integrity and live by it as our true selves.

In essence, it is to be *real*. To be true to who you really are and not who you think you should be. I believe you need to find the path meant for you. I think in many cases we try to emulate things that have no relation to our real world. We believe we should be like someone else. As Oscar Wilde said, "Be yourself. Everyone else is taken." Because trying to be something we are not leads to incongruity with our true selves and often results in dysfunction and issues with others. People can sense it. There is no quick fix to being a leader; there is no pill and no shortcut. It requires self-reflection and openness.

In the army, we would help leaders to engage in the mask of command. The mask of command is determining what the situation requires and then exhibiting that leadership trait for that moment. You cannot do that if you don't know who you are.

Understanding your strengths is about knowing what you are uniquely good at. We all have a unique skill set, but in my experience, perfectionism has kept many of my clients from acknowledging their individual skills. There is nothing more powerful and self-affirming than for those leaders who get 360-degree feedback and find that they are uniquely good

THE ENLIGHTENED LEADER: HOW TO LEAD PEOPLE

at what they do as leaders. Too often they are too busy being tough on themselves.

By the same token, we also need to know our limitations. I learned this the hard way. As a soldier, my job was to be able to shoot well. For me, this was one skill in thirty-four years that I never really mastered. As a young officer, I tried to hide my lack of shooting skills, but everyone knew. I was disingenuous and made a fool of myself by trying to look good at the thing I couldn't do well. I find that we often shy away from what we lack skills in. A classic case was a senior vice president who didn't have the technical skill required

> **Too often, we are unclear on what our goals in life are.**

for his work, so he shied away from exhibiting it. As a result, he annoyed his direct reports, and it eventually got him fired.

Too often we are unclear on what our goals in life are. As a result, we bounce along and then we wonder where our life went. I see this especially when someone loses their job. Until they know what they want and need, they never find the right job. If you ever find yourself in this predicament, go first to what you need and want rather than to the options that are out there. In our seminal training program, *The Leadership Path*, over a five-day period we get people to really think about what is important to them. We warn attendees that if you are not happy where you are, you will never be a good leader of that organization. As a result, some program participants return to their company only to leave it shortly afterward.

Authenticity and Ethics

Integrity is an important part of self-awareness, and integrity is about being whole with one's self. It is about not being torn asunder by competing demands. To avoid being torn, we need to understand our ethics. Ethics represent our purpose. Purpose is a reflection of intent. Purpose and thereby intention reflect our motivations, what we value, and our character. We aren't talking about goals here; we are talking about who we really are. The issue of ethics is huge because too often we see the examples of the opposite. I believe it starts by first understanding how we see others. In too many cases, we have witnessed the very human nature of sense of superiority. I see it all the time: "I have this title and you are beneath me." It just gets worse from there. You have to believe in people; otherwise, you will not respect them. I always believed as an officer that no one was beneath being treated with respect, but I have seen many cases in the business world and in the military where that sense of superiority got in the way. In leadership, it all starts with that ethical backbone and particularly in valuing everyone.

The best manifestation of valuing everyone is being able to listen to differing views. When you listen with attention to the opinions of others, you demonstrate that you are valuing others. Instead, what I have seen time and time again is the small person who cannot bear to be outed and who then takes on arrogant traits. Feeling superior is a form of being small, and it is inauthentic. Lack of authenticity generally manifests itself in three destructive traits that all interrelate.

❋ **FEELING LIKE AN IMPOSTER:** Yes, the imposter syndrome is alive and well. If I do not reflect on my beliefs and upbringing, I can feel like a pretender in my role. As a result, I don't fully engage and shy away in fulfilling my accountabilities.

❋ **LACK OF CONFIDENCE:** This can result from imposter syndrome, but without taking stock of my strengths and capabilities, how can I be truly confident? Again, I may not fully commit to my role as a leader. Furthermore, a lack of confidence can make me feel small in relation to others. This leads me to behave badly to others by either being overly challenging or overly controlling.

❋ **NOT LISTENING TO OTHERS:** Lack of confidence and imposter syndrome can lead me to not listen to others. I may not feel comfortable enough to be challenged and have my logic tested, so I create an awful place to work where others' opinions are ignored.

To be clear, I am also no saint and have lived by these three traits. It is hard to overcome these without being genuinely authentic.

Servant Leadership

The second element to the enlightened leader is servant leadership. There are a lot of books on this topic; it has become a bit faddish. My perspective on servant leadership comes from my earliest leadership training in the army. For me, the phrase that best denotes servant leadership is *leaders eat last*.

This is a concept instilled in junior officers from day one. The premise is that you need to take care of your team first because they do the heavy lifting for you. It is not about ego and power position; it is for the care and concern of your people.

> The premise is that you need to take care of your team first because they do the heavy lifting for you.

For example, we had to keep a platoon commander's notebook in which we had everyone's details, including the names of their family members and their hobbies, right down to their shoe size. We had to know and care about every aspect of the thirty-one soldiers under our command. All heady stuff for a twenty-year-old. To demonstrate accountability, the company commander would come around and inspect our notebooks to instill in us a sense of care for our people. We have adapted this same methodology to assist businesses. To use an old phrase of mine, what is not inspected is not respected.

Servant leadership is even more critical in this present age. We need to care because we rely on our people for our success and for the success of our mission. Too often leaders lose sight of this. As a client recently said about the thousands of employees working for her, "We need to know and care for everyone because everyone is struggling in some way or another right now." This is the more positive leadership form of being accountable for the output of your team that I discussed in chapter 3.

Our characterization of servant leadership is embodied

in our golden rule of leadership—know your people and promote their welfare. Honestly *know* what makes them tick and ensure that you understand them in detail. This rule that was instilled in me almost forty years ago has stayed with me throughout my professional life. We work to impart this essential truth into reality for each of our clients.

The Tenets of Servant Leadership

The successful servant leader lives by five tenets:

* Seek and accept responsibility.

* Ensure understanding of intent.

* Be the impediment remover.

* Encourage thinking and input.

* Understand your people.

SEEK AND ACCEPT RESPONSIBILITY

The first is to seek and accept responsibility for your team and lead them by example. Feeling responsible for your team is a critical tenet. Not only will you be held accountable, as I discussed earlier, but also you need to feel obliged to care for your team. Seeking responsibility is taking on things to better your team and every individual on it. If you do not value your team, it will be very hard to accept responsibility for the team. Personal obligation will make you go that extra mile to support your team. Again, their success is your success, and they will know and detect whether you have a sense of obligation toward them. In return you will get their loyalty and engagement.

ENSURE UNDERSTANDING OF INTENT

The second tenet may not appear servant-like, but it is crucial. **A servant leader ensures that their team truly understands their intent and direction.** It is about clarity. Taking the time to make sure your intention is understood enables the team to use their own thinking and ensures their success in their work. Too many times leaders' intentions are misunderstood. The classic line, "Hey, why don't we go get her?" is often misconstrued to be direction when the reality is that it was a suggestion, and suddenly thousands of ships are heading for Troy.

A CEO I worked with was constantly frustrated because his team always thought his musings were direction. As a result, needless work, toil, and effort were put into projects that were of no use to the business. The same goes for being clear in their direction. As Bill Jensen says in his book *Simplicity*[5], make sure they are clear on what you want them to know, how you want them to feel as a result, and what specifically you want them to do. If you do these three things, you will be clear. In workshops we ask people to review the last email they sent to their team. Were these three things clear? Because if they were not, you have forced your people into needless work.

---

5   Bill Jensen, *Simplicity* (New York: Harper Business, 2000).

BE AN IMPEDIMENT REMOVER

The second tenet leads into the third: become an impediment remover. The servant leader focuses their energy on clearing the road for their team. It requires stealth. This is a form of practicing continuous improvement, but it is structured around the leader understanding the things getting in the way of their team members' success. In servant leadership, we pave the way for our teams. Obstacle clearance is an art. It requires asking what the impediments to success are. But it also requires not just taking the monkey on the leader's back and fixing it but helping them to fix it so that they are more self-sufficient next time. This requires coaching, not

> In servant leadership, we pave the way for our teams. Obstacle clearance is an art. It requires asking what the impediments to success are.

just fixing. Too many times out of our care and concern for our team, we take away learning opportunities because we want to be the hero, and we want them to like us. This is where the art comes into it. How you help them through it is the art. The science is always looking for the impediments. It goes back to the pain points discussed earlier. Removing the pain helps people to embrace change, so helping them to help themselves will move them forward. The very real human impediment, though, is fear. The leader's role is to remove fear. In many cases, fear emanates from risk, and leaders need to get really good at embracing risk and managing it. Helping others to embrace the riskiness of life and work is the real value of leaders.

An equation (which is not really an equation) from Tim Gallwey's *The Inner Game of Tennis* is performance equals potential minus interference:[6]

$$P = p - i$$

The leader removes the interferences that get in the way and inhibit performance. They recognize the potential in everyone, and they work to enable it. Sometimes those interferences have to do with confidence and sometimes with fear that we must be masters at dealing with all of these imposters as leaders.

ENCOURAGE THINKING AND INPUT

The fourth tenet is to encourage your team's thinking and input. **You need their thinking and their input because they are closest to the action.** This tenet relies on the art of asking, not telling. Questions launch peoples' thinking, and the best leaders get good at asking questions. This ties back to your self-awareness because others may have radically different ideas from you. You will need to be aware of how much diversion from the norm you can handle because they may take you there. This dovetails nicely into the accountability for best advice. If you are asking them questions, you will be able to very quickly build trust for them to be open and honest with you, and you will get the better best advice. Asking questions and encouraging thinking is all about diversity and inclusion.

Thinking is the ultimate diversity.

---

6   W. Timothy Gallwey, *The Inner Game of Tennis* (New York: Random House Trade Paperbacks, 1997).

Thinking is the ultimate diversity. In my twenty-five years of working with Effective Intelligence and profiling people's thinking, I have never found two people in the same organization with the exact same profile. This means that we all see the exact same things but we process them differently. It means that we all have different ideas and opinions. So a servant leader needs to encourage thinking and hear the thinking of others. Unlocking thinking and its manifestation, communication, is the force multiplier on the modern corporate battlefield. You need them both, and the servant leader values the diverse thinking of others and shows their inclusiveness by listening. It demonstrates that you value them and what they have to say. If the vast majority of our paychecks are for our thinking, then you had better get good at encouraging thinking.

UNDERSTAND YOUR PEOPLE

The final tenet is to fully understand your people and in so doing always maintain or enhance their self-esteem. Understanding your people requires knowing their capability. Understanding your people means knowing your people. In regard to knowing everything about them, I believe the 80/20 rule must apply. You don't need to know some things, but there is probably a lot you don't already know. Knowing your people enables you to promote their welfare by not putting them in situations that will damage them. The worst mistake a leader can make is to damage the self-esteem of their people. Making people feel small does not make you big. I experienced firsthand what diminishing self-esteem looks and feels like in my army basic training and then again in basic officer training. It can be very damaging. The days of the abusive drill sergeant in Hollywood movies are over. There are other ways to build the team, and they are not at the expense of the individual. It is what makes for good teamwork. Again, it is about maintaining and enhancing self-esteem and not diminishing it.

Too often, though, we don't practice servant leadership. In many cases, it is because we are *not* authentic leaders. Instead, we are driven by our ego and our desire to control people. Servant leaders need humility. You are performing a critical role to unleash the potential of your people. Personal interferences will prevent you from being successful. The biggest personal interference is leadership hubris.

Hubris: The Anathema of Servant Leadership

Hubris is excessive pride or overconfidence, and unfortunately it is all too common in managerial leadership. It is a poison that infects teams and destroys trust. It's important to remember that its origins are in Greek tragedy, leading to nemesis or ultimately downfall. Hubris also signals a disconnect or a loss of connection with reality. Leaders who aren't aware of what their organizations are doing lower down are guilty of hubris. Leaders who don't cascade their strategy and intent farther down are creating hubris for themselves. It also shows up as arrogance and all too often as a desire to find faults in others while ignoring our own. That hubris (or arrogance that they are the only ones who *know*) is what causes leaders to fall into the tyranny of do. It is that hubris that causes leaders to dive down in work. Hubris can be shortsightedness after a period of success, so long-term planning and goals can combat it. I believe that its roots are threefold:

* **FACADE:** The need to maintain an exterior image to keep others at bay and maintain our status. We know deep inside (consciously or not) that we have flaws, but we need to keep up those appearances.

* **PERFECTIONISM:** The misbegotten belief that perfection is attainable and that I am either there or striving for it. Perfectionism is the surest route to unhappiness because it is unachievable.

* **LACK OF CONFIDENCE:** The root of demonstrating overconfidence is actually to lack real confidence. Although this may appear at odds with the definition, it is the core cause of the other two.

While nemesis is seen as an inescapable demise, hubris can be controlled before it becomes fatal. We can come to grips with our own fallibility through self-awareness and reflection and lead a happier life. Humility is the other ingredient that is essential and critical for leaders. As soon as we realize, deep down inside, that we are flawed beings, we can break the stigma of hubris. As soon as we see ourselves as no better than anyone else, we have achieved humility. As Kipling said, "If you can walk with the crowd and keep your virtue, or walk with

Kings—nor lose the common touch."[7] We are all human, and we all make mistakes. I have made thousands of mistakes in my life but hopefully not the one of lacking humility.

Humility as a concept gets a bad rap. It doesn't mean rending your garments and exposing all your weaknesses or being self-effacing; it means being grounded in respect, tolerance, and mutually beneficial understandings for the organization and the individual. I believe it is about trust in those you hired to do the work you hired them to do. Trust in your strategy (that you are cascading properly) and your willingness to accept best advice from those who have the expertise. Humility is not resting on your laurels but rather by doing that farsighted and future-looking evaluation of yourself.

For leaders, this is so important because people will only follow you so far. They will follow your hubris just so they can watch you fall from grace, but they aren't really following *you*. Our job as leaders is to deliver the strategy while positively impacting others. In other words, we have a moral imperative to create great places to work where people flourish and reach their full potential. That will not happen if we believe we are better than them. A humble leader doesn't lack vision or confidence; they just recognize that business is a team effort and that constant learning is needed. It is forward propulsion and not the inertia of hubris.

Too often when I see hubris in action, it is clear to me that it is the failing of a leader in that employee's life. Perhaps

---

7   Rudyard Kipling, *Rewards and Fairies* (London: Doubleday, Page & Co., 1910).

anaklesis got in the way and they were too worried to take it on, or they just thought it was too much work. Such a leader does no service to that employee in the long run. The leader of leaders must step up. How much better would our world be if this were the case? As Viscount Field Marshal Lord Slim said, "Moral courage is higher and rarer value than physical courage." It needs to be grown and nurtured.

Transformational Leadership

The final element of the enlightened leader is transformational leadership. Transformational leadership is leading through a vision of a better place. It is about stepping out of the reality of what is now and looking to the future. These days are about seeing the need to change and improve and taking the time now to do it.

> Transformational leadership is leading through a vision of a better place. It is about stepping out of the reality of what is now and looking to the future.

Its roots are summed up by the direction I received when I took command of a new team, unit, or formation—to leave it in a better state than you found it. It wasn't good enough to achieve your goals; it was about making things better. At its source is the notion of continuous improvement. The exercise of leadership over others is always an exercise of continuous improvement.

Our job as leaders is to help people get better and transform themselves and, therefore, our organizations. Organizations don't change because we decree we need more of this and less of that; they change by the efforts of energetic human beings. Leaders who do not understand this are destined to be very disappointed indeed.

Build Your People

What annoys me these days is the assumption that many leaders can get to their goals by hiring better people. They don't realize that their work is to transform the people they already have and help them grow in their careers, not be tossed on a slag heap because they can't hit the goal right now or, god forbid, they made a mistake. Integral to transformational leadership is learning from mistakes and allowing for errors. Transformation doesn't come from a perfectionist mindset but rather from a growth mindset that sees people learning along the way. Therefore, to practice transformational leadership, you need to be authentic and clear on your foibles, and you need to be a servant leader to help your people.

TRANSFORMATIONAL LEADERSHIP DEFINED

Transformational leadership is about being the change agent for your organization. It is about change that creates great places to work. Leaders who transform do the following:

* Have a vision and lead by it.

* Develop the leadership potential of their direct reports.

✳ Inspire a desire in others by example.

✳ Manage the tension between the current state and the future goals.

In short, they point the way by breathing life into others. They don't get caught in the reality loop. Instead, they choose to look toward the possibilities of a better future. Transformational leadership is about inspiring. Just like breathing life into others, it is done by the example we set. Inspiring them is essential; it will give them the breath of air to deal with the stressors coming at them. If we can do it, we will in turn gain their confidence and trust.

Leadership by Example

Often in workshops I ask people what it means to lead by example. People talk about it all the time, but very few live by it. The answers to this question are usually spot-on, but there is a disconnect. The behaviors don't match the words. I recently watched with horror in the age of the coronavirus when the head of employee safety chose to ignore his CEO's edict to wear masks in the room. I believe part of the problem is because leaders don't understand and practice the other two forms of enlightened leadership: authentic and servant. If I don't know what is important to me, I can't demonstrate it and thereby inspire others. If I don't fully embrace being a servant to my people, I will not inspire them.

Being the Enlightened Leader

In *The Leadership Path* program, we challenge our participants to write their story, which becomes their personal brand and is an expression of enlightened leadership. We get senior directors and vice presidents to reflect on their purpose and what they are trying to create. The exercise of reflection helps them to get in touch with their true selves. It gets them to explore the threads that hold them to their current world. From there they determine to either strengthen or cut those threads. Their story requires them to dig deep into who they are to enable them to be authentic, servant, and transformational leaders. We ask them to be able to answer these questions:

- **WHO AM I?** What unique experiences have impacted them to make them behave the way they do?

- **WHY AM I HERE?** What is their purpose and the purpose of their work?

- **WHAT AM I TRYING TO BUILD?** When they leave here, what is their legacy, and what teachable point of view have they created for others?

Developing your story will help you to launch your intentions. As we said before, people have changed, and no doubt you have as well. Leadership is all about aligning people to a common direction, but first you need to start with yourself.

So take the time and ask yourself, "Do I live by this credo?" Do your leaders live by this philosophy, or are they just collecting paychecks? As part of the enlightened leader, authentic and servant leadership are mindsets and must be practiced with a disciplined approach. The next question to ask yourself is, "Do my leaders think this way?" We don't have to transform the whole organization; we merely have to change our team. As I ask every leader when they take over a new team, "What will be your legacy in three years?" The enlightened leader is part of the profession of managerial leadership. It is the ethos that the leader uses to infuse their management skills. A critical role for your enlightened leaders is ensuring that their leaders are looking to the mental health of their people. Business needs to understand that, by and large, the work is done by human beings. That humanness means we need to ensure our employees' physical, social, and psychological health.

> It is in our power to stop the slide and create that great place to work.

The leader of leaders is attuned to and focused upon enlightened leadership. If you have ever experienced those in a leadership role who don't exercise enlightened leadership, it is because those leaders of leaders did not lead the way. They did not mold their leaders and again provided a disservice to them. But I firmly believe it is never too late. It is in our power to stop the slide and create that great place to work.

Milestone #5: Enlightened Leadership

This milestone on your journey will require much more reflection than others. It is about getting into your own soul and pondering the souls of your direct report leaders. You also need to explore the soul of your organization. Will it bear the weight of being enlightened and release the human power of the organization? In the next stage of our journey, we will explore the nature of how management and leadership come together and what work needs to be done to push you, your teams, and your organization forward.

Reflect on great leaders in your life. How enlightened were they?

How so, and how not so?

What do you notice?

How authentic a leader are you?

What needs more work?

What will you do about it?

Consider your leaders. How authentic are they?

Which need to focus on this?

What will you do about it?

How much of a servant leader are you?

Why?

What will you do?

Consider your leaders. Who are more servant oriented, and who are not?

Which need to focus on this skill and why?

What will you do about it?

How much of a transformational leader are you?

Why?

What will you do about it?

Consider your leaders. Who are more transformational, and who are not?

Which need to focus more on this skill and why?

What will you do about it?

What is the state of hubris and humility in your team?

How do you know?

What will you do about it?

CHAPTER 6

STRATEGY OPERATIONS AND TACTICS: THE FOCUS OF WORK

No plan survives first contact. That isn't a reason
not to plan; it is just about adaptability.

The Operational Art

In 1922, Marshal Tukhachevsky of the Soviet Army introduced a concept that would have an impact on soldiering for
over one hundred years. The Soviets were coming out of the
Russian Revolution and struggling with the tension of two
constructs regarding how to conduct warfare. For almost a
century before, there was a strategic level that achieved the
aims of the country, and there were tactics of the immediate

battlefield where the fighting was raging that enabled lower levels to achieve their goals. The problem was that there was something missing. There was a middle range missing between the lofty aims of strategy and the action-oriented, in-the-moment elements of tactics. Tukhachevsky identified the need for the middle layer, and it became known as the operational art. Operations were the ways to achieve the strategy but at a level above the tactical. This operational art became key to the successes of the Red Army against the Nazis in the Second World War. In subsequent postwar years as NATO tried to deal with the menace of the Soviet Union in Western Europe, the forces began to explore the nature of the operational art and adopted the concepts. So how NATO looks at the strategic, operational, and tactical is that at the strategic level, it would be NATO's role to protect the North Atlantic Treaty nations. The operational level would be NATO extending that to operations in Afghanistan as a way to protect the treaty nations, and the tactical would be the activities in certain provinces in Afghanistan to enable control of Afghanistan.

The Operational Art in Business

For me, the most important part of the operational art was the linkage between strategy and tactics. As I have suggested, *strategy* is a word with many different meanings to many different people. It gets caught up in describing a level, a nature of activity, and defining what something ought to be. Too many times in my career as an executive coach, I have been presented with the phrase that "this person needs to be more strategic." The problem then was to define what they mean by that. It has often led to confusion for the coaching client and for myself—what was really necessary for them to do in their role, and what did they really mean by "be more strategic"?

An example of the differences between the levels in business is that strategy would be Disney in the film business. The operational would be the studio heads and departments, and the tactical would be the specific movies that are made.

Strategy in Business

As mentioned before, the term *strategic* is often used to denote higher-level planning. Far too often the word has cachet. It is far sexier to use the word *strategy* than the more mundane *planning*. If I am working on strategy, it feels bigger than just planning. This is because, after all, *plan* is only a four-letter word and not worthy of real effort.

Tactics in Business

Tactics for business have been very much "how we do things" and are used to represent what happens at the lower levels in the organization where the execution is essential. Again, there is almost a scornful view taken of tactics to represent what happens among the workers. Tactics are very much how we do things, and strategy represents what we are trying to achieve. While there is often a passing reference to executive-level tactics, it is not really their work. The real issue is that although there is an innate sense of these words, they are laden with subjective meaning.

In reality, there is a gap between lofty strategy and the undignified, unassuming, and ordinary tactics. Tactics don't really represent the ways and means to achieve strategy. In business parlance, what was missing for me was describing the ways and means to achieve the grand objectives. As a result, I have spent considerable time helping organizations understand the nature of those ways and means as the operations. It is interesting to note that the root word of tactics is *taktos* in Greek, which means "ordered or arranged," so tactics are really about *organizing for achieving goals,* whereas strategy comes from the byzantine word for *general.* The essence of both these words is that they represent setting a level, which is a very important thinking skill. It is about looking at the work through levels and not just categories. Setting a level is choosing the appropriate level to work at.

But if strategy is at the top and tactics is the orderly way to achieve goals, then *there needs to be something in between.* This becomes real for business because there is often a strategy that disconnects from the actions at the lower levels. The generals (the executives) identify where they want to be and then leave it up to the levels below to figure out how. We have had several clients who have struggled to move from the lofty ideals of organizational direction to *making it happen.* Too many times I have sat in executive sessions where the top says, "This is where we want to be" and then just expects that the work will get done through systems and processes farther down. The problem with all of this is that there are distinct levels that need to be thought through, and there are roles and structure that must be able to translate what needs to be done. The translation is about taking the abstract strategic objectives and putting them into mechanical terms that leaders can then use to *achieve* those objectives.

The Operational Level in Business

The operational level then becomes the ways and means to achieve the strategy, and the tactics become the systems to deliver the goals. Its role is to make tactical actions serve strategic ends. It is about linking the abstraction of high-level thinking into a coherent

> The operational level then becomes the ways and means to achieve the strategy, and the tactics become the systems to deliver the goals.

approach that is not random and has a greater chance of success. Our clients have found this valuable in an integrated planning process that starts with strategy, then determines the operations to achieve the goals, and finally defines the methods and processes to achieve the goals. Planning from top to bottom is essential, and it needs to be integrated.

Marshal Tukhachevsky's operational art represents another method for business to look at the ways and means to achieve the strategy. The militaries of the world explore the operational art much deeper, and it denotes structures as opposed to constructs, as I am suggesting. In my experience, the best example of not understanding the nature of the operational art is in organizational structure.

Case in point: A client of ours felt the need to reduce headcount and determined that the best way to do that was to take out levels in the organization. They understood that there was a strategic level that defined direction and where the business needed to go. They also saw that there was very much an action-oriented level that oversaw the execution and made the real work happen. Respectively, these were the vice president level and the manager levels. As a result, they removed the director level because they didn't understand the connectivity between strategy and tactics. Great savings were achieved initially and then they suddenly found that things fell apart. The messages got lost in translation; they created the gaps. If you ever played the telephone game as a child, you can imagine just how broken those messages got. The grand scheme of what the business wanted to be was lost, and there was no planning on how to make that real for the front line. The end result was that they paid *twice*, once to remove the level and then again to hire the level back. While this is a simple example, it demonstrates a lack of understanding of the need for a level between strategy and tactics.

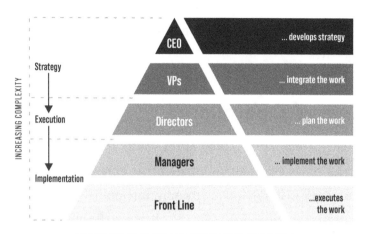

STRATEGY OPERATIONS AND TACTICS AT LEVELS

To this day, some businesses see this relationship in a purely binary nature. There are only strategy and tactics. What they miss is that there is a true art that lies in between. It is that ability to develop the objectives—the ways and means to achieve the strategy. I believe this is actually what has created the preponderance in strategy titles in organizations as people try to describe work that feels bigger than tactics but that is not the core corporate strategy.

> The art is the ability to define the objectives that, once accumulated, achieve the strategy but also describe the ways and means to get there.

The art is the ability to define the objectives that, once accumulated, achieve the strategy but also describe the ways and means to get there. With our clients in planning, we describe these as the lines of operation to achieve objectives.

These lines can be things like sales, technology, or customer service. They are about determining the route to get to the objectives.

Lines of Operation

While the output of getting to the routes is a linear process, the key is working backward from the objectives to define what needs to be done along the way. Interestingly, the human being is the only creature on the planet that can do this. This ability is working from an end state or goal back to where they are now. This is a uniquely human thing, and it is core to planning.

> While the output of getting to the routes is a linear process, the key is working backward from the objectives to define what needs to be done along the way.

Too often, though, we start from where we are now and move forward in our thinking. While simpler and satisfying, it does not help you to achieve your objective. Too many times plans are comprised of where we are now, to which we add X percent. These are not plans; they are goals.

PLANNING VERSUS LIFE

At the operational level, planning is a critical skill to hone. So many strategies fail because this work is not done. When we teach planning, it is amazing how few understand its nature. Too often planning is *where are we now* plus *what we want to add*. This signifies that the thinking work has not been done. We aren't planning; we are working the plan, as shown in the previous figure. This approach also adds organizational pain because we are adding work while not really determining what work is no longer needed or a priority. This is often why our employees feel overloaded.

The essence of the operational art is to create the understanding of the importance of the operational level. Not only does it have an element of how it is thought through and planned but also it represents the nature of work for managerial leaders. This is the most important point that business can take from understanding the operational art.

The importance is that it represents the managerial work that occurs to ensure organizational success. The operational level starts with managers of managers. Given that most businesses are really only five levels, the operational level is only at the third level, or the first level of managers' managers.

Whereas in an organization with several true business units, the operational level is the first level of managers of managers and the next level. For a level-six organization, these represent the director and the vice president level, respectively. For the grand businesses that focus on the ability to align their corporate effort with the global future, or what we call a level-seven organization, the operational level is still two levels, the director and the vice president. This is because the executive vice president level needs to be strategic to enable the business units. In other words, the strategy level is the realm of the executive, but the operational level is everything between the executive and the frontline management. These levels are the most critical to the success of the organization. If these levels are not working well, then you will know by the problems and issues that arise within months.

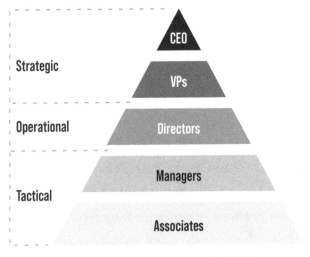

LEVEL 5 ORGANIZATION

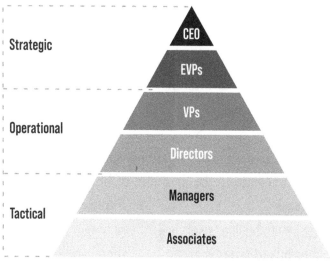

LEVEL 6 ORGANIZATION

LEVEL 7 ORGANIZATION

The Operational Art and Innovation

There is another element that the operational level is critical for: innovation. *Innovation* is one of those overused words with little clarity of meaning. Let's go back to its roots: *in*, meaning "to bring in," and *nova*, meaning "new." So innovation is defined here as bringing new things into the organization or the market. The operational level is the starting point of real innovation. The first level of bringing new ideas or implementing is at the manager level, where there are opportunities for process improvement.

> The key to business survival in turbulent times is at the operational level.

As an example, the next level in a simple manufacturing business develops the innovation at the operational level, which is product improvement. In financial services it is systems improvement. It is important to understand that the difference is not the ideation but the accountability to find the opportunities.

The ideas can come from anywhere, but the thinking to put them into place needs to be done at the appropriate level. The key to business survival in turbulent times is at the operational level. Many of our clients now understand that while effectiveness, efficiency, and trust were critical to success, adaptability has become king in changing markets. As the ways and means begin to level, the operational levels find the ways and means to develop new approaches. They seek the alternate pathways to achieve the strategy and think in terms of what contingencies need to be put in place if something new happens. This is the first level of deep thought to the challenges of the business in order to find the new ways. It is the first level that addresses organizational pain to try to remove the interferences in the organizational potential with a view to making things better.

INNOVATION AT LEVELS	
LEVEL 6	Designed Corporate Strategy Change
LEVEL 5	Opportunity for Corporate Strategy Change
LEVEL 4	Designed Product Improvement
LEVEL 3	Opportunity for Product Improvement
LEVEL 2	Designed Continuous Improvement
LEVEL 1	Opportunity for Continuous Improvement

Here is a visual representation to consider. The operational level is the linking pin for the strategy. As an analogy, it is like the trailer hitch on the back of the truck. The truck itself is the strategy driving to a particular point. The operational level is the hitch that connects the tactical trailer. It controls and directs the tactical level by connecting it to the strategy. Without that trailer hitch, the strategy truck goes on, the tactics grind to a halt, and nothing is achieved.

What is often missed is the understanding of the expectation of that operational level. Too many times this failure of understanding leads that level to either try to reach up and be strategic or, more often, to be very tactical. The manifestation of being too tactical is that they compress the managers at the tactical level. The manager questions what they are doing and how they are doing it, demanding that it be done a certain way or that it's going to be their way or the highway. This results in micromanagement of getting into the details or the weeds and not choosing the right level to operate from. This in turn is very dissatisfying for the managers at the tactical level. They are over-monitored and questioned on every aspect of their work. In my experience, too often these managers who are compressing the tactical level believe they are really adding value to their direct reports, but in reality they are not working at the level expected of them. At the other extreme, where they are too focused on the strategic level and not linking the real strategy, they are not working at level either. It is very rare that they focus upward into the strategic realm. In my experience, the preponderance is to work at the tactical level where there is comfort and a greater sense of accomplishment. The longer-term impact is that compressed managers disengage or try to find other things to do, and in those rare occasions where they are at too high a level, they will leave because they feel unfulfilled.

There are two culprits here. The first is a lack of understanding of the operational level and its importance to the organization. Far too often level-five organizations and above don't really understand the level of director and denigrate it. It often has no definition of its distinction from the manager level, so the incumbent knows no better. But the incumbent is not the issue. In reality, the manager of the director level in question is the real culprit. The manager at that level is again the one who does not define the expectation and hold the team accountable to do the work. But then they couldn't know to do so if they didn't understand the true nature of managerial leadership and the nature of levels.

It is all well and good to define a level, but the reality lies in the actions of the human beings involved. This is where the operational level needs to come alive. It is the role of middle management to bring this operational level to life. Understanding the nature of their various roles has to start at the top and cascade down. The rationale for this is that the strategic level defines the framework for the operational level, but more importantly it holds them accountable to implement it. This cannot rely just on a director's personal sense of obligation. Doing so introduces risk, so while the operational level of work belongs to a certain level, that level needs to be held to account to perform the function. They cannot be held to account if the directors and vice presidents don't understand the construct or are not held to account by their own managers to ensure that the operational level is exercised effectively.

Getting Good at the Operational Art

As a manager of managers, the critical takeaway is that there are these various levels, and you have to have different expectations for what happens at the operational and tactical levels.

> To be effective at the operational level, you must understand the strategy as it applies to you and be able to translate that to the level below.

To be effective at the operational level, you must understand the strategy as it applies to you and be able to translate that to the level below. What this level needs is understanding and context in order to be truly effective in designing operations.

Share Knowledge

Too often the information that is necessary is *not* provided. This is described as holding out or hoarding information. In my experience, there are many who believe that they are being kept in the dark deliberately. The refrain is that knowledge is power. There is a misbegotten belief that leaders and managers alike hold back information. I have heard on many occasions that management likes to "keep us in the dark." In all my experiences, this is really the farthest from the truth. I acknowledge that it can seem this way, but this is not necessarily the case. I refer to this as being an act of omission rather than an act of commission. An act of omission is an oversight or an opportunity missed. An act of commission is a deliberate act perpetrated for a subjective reason. Far too often we misconstrue our leaders' intent and assume that their actions were deliberate. In my experience, it was not about a leader's intention but rather an error or a missed chance to do something. I have yet to find cases where people really held back the important information to plan.

Clarify Context

An understanding of organizational context is critical to success at this level. The managers at this level need to have insight into not only their boss's plans but also much more of what the situational context is. They need this to better plan the operational level but also to be ready to adapt. An example of this is when a change occurs at the top of the organization, the last level to be concerned or interested in the change is this operational level. Too many times there is a belief that these changes will be *felt* by the tactical level, but this is never really the case. They are too far removed and nor should they be concerned. The tactical level is all about execution; they need to get on with the real work value for the organization.

The Impact of Speed of Change

Another important issue to the effectiveness of the operational level is the drive at the strategic level to change and actions. Far too many times, the operational level finds themselves compressed to action by the levels above. For example, there was no way to move the *Titanic* from its trajectory to the iceberg, as it was a being in motion and the path was set. It is the same for organizations. The strategic level

> Far too many times, the operational level finds themselves compressed to action by the levels above.

must plan out farther to enable the operational level to plan and organize the tactical level. You need to steer away earlier or adjust to a point where you can still attain the right trajectory. We live in an age of instant everything. But the strategic level needs to give the operational level the time to do their work rather than expecting instant action at the tactical level. In my experience, this is why the operational level often fails. They don't have the time to put in place what is necessary. It causes them to compress and force actions at the next level. While this may work in that particular moment, it is unsustainable. Our clients who have been successful have had an epiphany—first that there is an operational level and second that it needs time to perform its role. These successful clients have overcome their tyranny of do and spend more time thinking ahead and exploring what might be out there.

Universal Translation Again

The final role that this level performs is that of the universal translator. As the translator of strategy, this role must be able to take the elements of the strategy and make it real for the levels below. It not only is a case of cascading the strategy but also is about clarifying what the elements of the strategy mean. What does the vision mean to the execution level? What is the implication of the application of the values at the tactical level, and what does the mission mean to this level?

> Translation of the strategy means putting it in words and language for the most important level of the organization—the tactical execution level.

Translation of the strategy means putting it in words and language for the most important level of the organization—the tactical execution level. The bottom two levels are the most important to your organization. It is at these levels that the real work gets done. It is usually where the bulk of the employees are, and these people represent the real leadership challenge to the business. Here is where the employees need to be engaged and focused on the work. Ironically, it is also the lowest-paid level, and too many times, it is looked down upon with scorn by those in the ivory towers. The operational level needs to understand its important role in connecting the business and that those directors or vice presidents are not there for their own edification but to connect the execution for the business. Again, the failure of the operational level to translate the strategy has meant a disconnection. This manifests itself because it feels to all levels like the executives are not aligned and that the strategy is always changing. This is particularly the case when there is little or no context given for changes that occur.

Our best clients have developed a new respect for the operational level and now ensure that they have the context to be successful. They also fully understand that they must give this level the time they need to steer the ship. It is the operational level that takes the helm of the ship. The captains can set the direction, but the helmsmen steer the efforts of the stokers and the engine room to get there.

While Tukhachevsky was trying to solve for the issues of battle, the modern business leader can take a page from his book and adapt their understanding of how organizations need to work.

Milestone #6: The Operational Art

At this milestone in your journey, it is time to really assess the operational level of your organization. To do that, you must explore strategy, operations, and tactics. The questions will help you consider the implications of the levels on the planning work that you and your managers need to do. If you are at the operational level in your organization, what insight does your boss need? In the next chapter, we will explore the specific skills you must possess, and more importantly for the manager of managers, the skills you need to develop in your managers.

How clear is your strategy?

How well is it articulated and referred to?

What do you need to do differently?

Are your ways and means to achieve the strategy clear?

How do you know?

What will you do about it?

How good are your tactics?

Are your processes clear?

Is it clear how the work flows?

How effective is your operational level?

Do they have the time to plan?

Do the tactical levels have time to plan?

How clear is the context for others?

How good is your situational awareness?

What will you do about it?

How well do you set priorities?

How well do your subordinate managers set priorities?

What will you do about it?

How good are you at innovation?

Are you hearing ideas coming from below?

What will you do about it?

Do your people live by the values?

Do your managers drive home the values?

What will you do about it?

How effective is your knowledge management?

Do your people share information well?

What are the opportunities to improve knowledge sharing?

CHAPTER 7

SKILLS OF MANAGERIAL LEADERSHIP

Skills are the sum total of our lives; every moment of our journey builds them.

In the realm of leadership development, there is much emphasis placed on skill building. Learning leadership and management is seen as a skill-building exercise. Often there is a premium placed on learning a tactical skill. Something that I can get my hands around, something that I have to practice doing, such as turning widgets or building a house frame. Recently I had one of those sessions with an executive team that felt that they had been ripped off—why didn't we learn how to do something tangible like have a tough conversation? I call this oppression *behavioralism*. There is a level and a place for learning specific tactical skills. But once you are in the C-suite, you had better not be looking for tactics. "Show me how to do it" may be a shortcut to development, but it provides me with a safety blanket. The oppression of behavioralism is that a set of behaviors is best suited here, such as, "If X happens, then I do B. If Y happens, I do D." Leading people is not about these shallow tactics. At the level of managerial leader of managerial leaders, it requires a different set of skills. There is no magic formula, and your managers need to understand this reality. It cannot be formulaic. As I have said, it is a lifelong learning. Those sets of skills are about thinking. When I am in front of people, I am working to help them to *think* better. The managerial leader of managerial leaders needs to be able to think through their work and how they will manage and lead.

> There is no magic formula, and your managers need to understand this reality. It cannot be formulaic.

Thinking: The Undiscovered Country

When I talk about thinking, I am not using the constrained definition of Myers and Briggs relegated to one facet of personality. What I mean is, How do you use your *whole self* in order to do something? It is interesting to ask a roomful of adults how much of their paycheck is for their *thinking*. The look of stunned silence is priceless. Strangely, it seems that no one has ever asked the question. The follow-up is then, Wouldn't it make sense for you to get better at it? Wouldn't it be worthwhile to get your managerial leaders thinking better? It is an interesting premise that our education system does not teach us how to think but rather *what* to think. The oppression of behavioralism is a form of teaching what to think. Teaching me how to have the difficult conversation is not about thinking it through but about just giving the techniques. It is inevitably a shortcut. Many clients ask for this type of training. They see their people as needing a skill set when what they really need is to understand that their role is to have the tough conversations. But they need to think differently about those conversations first.

THINKING DRIVES ACTION

Thinking drives thoughts. Thinking is how we use data to reach conclusions, and thoughts are the conclusions we reach. Once we have reached those conclusions, then our actions become our behaviors. The problem is that we are short-circuiting the system with the oppression of behavioralism. This lesson was proven to me many years ago while I was helping a leader who was having difficulty connecting with his direct reports. "I did just what you said. I read back what they said and answered their questions with questions, but it didn't work, and now they are even more disenchanted with me." What had happened was that they had merely put a plaster on their inability to connect. They had gone through the skill lessons and applied them, but they weren't authentic in their attempts. In reality, they didn't value the input or perspective of anyone else, and the team sensed it.

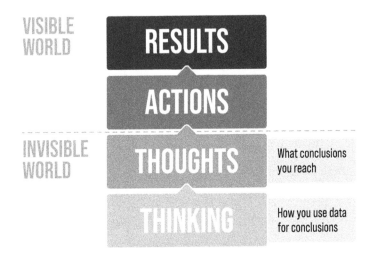

THINKING DRIVES RESULTS

The real trick here for the effective leader is to be able to think differently. Effective thinking is the thinking that gets things done. Take a simple thinking task like decision-making. Decision-making is about choosing one thing and rejecting all others. Regrettably, in our education system, we are not taught how to make a decision but rather what the decision should be. The core of our day-to-day work as employees is to make decisions. Yet decision-making is one of the major pain points for organizations. How is this possible?

> Effective thinking is the thinking that gets things done.

I believe it is built around three issues. They revolve around the fact that we are not taught how to make decisions. Mom and Dad teach us right from wrong. We learn that putting our hand on a hot stove is not a good decision. But people do not have a framework for the most fundamental thinking processes for human beings—that of decision-making. This is core to our problems and the three reasons why decision-making does not happen. If we don't have a framework, can we trust our choices? If we don't have a framework, will others trust the choices we make? And the final key management issue: Whose decision is it anyway? If any of these three issues are in play, it is easy to see why decision-making is pain.

If you layer on top of this the issue that we have preferences in where we direct our thinking, it results in decision-making being a really messy situation. Some of us are prejudiced; we make choices without all the facts. Others get caught in analysis paralysis and can't make choices and then still others see that there are never-ending ideas to be explored, kind of like the proverbial nutty professor where nothing comes to fruition. When faced with all of these factors in our thinking, it is no wonder that a junior manager once said to me, "It is surprising we are still afloat as an organization."

THINKING IS WORK

Being good at thinking does not come easily. It requires hard work. To get people to use a framework is hard. You are first asking them to change and overcome their anaklesis. Then you are asking them to use a foreign process. Instead, we like our comfort zone, and we like what we are used to. Thinking differently requires work and effort. Perhaps it is that we have been spoon-fed what to think for so long. To ask people to think differently goes even further because it requires us to know the kind of thinking we are engaging in and the other kind of thinking we need to do. Thinking differently is about learning a new language; it is about consciously focusing and immersing yourself in it. The new language will be necessary for the future. As humanity goes forward with technology, new thinking will be required even more. To think differently, you need discipline. As we have already seen, discipline in society is a rare thing.

THE MANAGERIAL LEADER ROLE IN THINKING

If these factors are all going against human nature, then it is time that we reintroduce the role of the managerial leader. When faced with these challenges, we need a coach to help us. This is the role of our boss. But there is a danger here. The coach/manager is potentially a victim of the same issues. The leader needs to challenge their own thinking in order to be an effective resource to their people. They suffer from the same issues: lack of framework and thinking bias. So the first skills that we need to hone are the skills to challenge our own thinking and the thinking of others.

CHALLENGING THINKING

Challenging thinking is to question the normal and the ways that things are being done. As an aside, it is the foundation to continuous improvement and to constructs like Kaizen. For the success of our organizations, we need to be able to question the sacred cows and most notably our thinking approaches. The greatest coaches push us to challenge our thinking frames to take us to new levels. An Olympic coach, for example, would fail miserably if they just accepted where the athlete saw themselves. The leadership coach needs to do the same—*challenge people to think differently.*

Like the authentic leader, the leader in this case needs to have an understanding of their thinking style and its impact on their effectiveness. We must critically assess to ensure that we are doing our best thinking and that our people are doing their best possible thinking. The question to ask them is, Are you sure you can't, or are you sure you can? If you ask this question, you have launched them onto the path of thinking as they formulate a response in their mind. Questioning thinking is not just telling them to do something; rather, it is enabling them to explore for themselves. It might be the same answer you would have gotten before, or it may be a brilliant new insight. By asking them the question, you have launched their thinking. It is not you telling them what to do. The greatest leaders for me have been those who asked great questions. At Forrest & Company, we train our coaches to ask the questions. We train them in the frameworks of decision-making or selling your ideas to help their clients achieve extraordinary results.

A final benefit to launching thinking is that it then becomes a lesson in and of itself, and gradually the muscle memory kicks in for sustained results. A CEO I work with truly understands the thinking of his team. He challenges them when he needs to, and at the same time, he has a great understanding of why they do what they do. He knows how he can redirect their energies to get the best out of them.

I would argue that the most important skill for managerial leaders is thinking. But to help them to think better, they need guidance. They need their boss to help them explore and imagine. They need their manager to help them to experience, analyze, rationalize, and evaluate. If there is one skill you need to hone, it should be thinking and working to develop strong thinking skills in others.

> If there is one skill you need to hone, it should be thinking and working to develop strong thinking skills in others.

Leader Self-Care

Another skill set that is just beginning to gain credence is a leader's self-care, and it starts with thinking. It is caring for yourself as an effective managerial leader to enable you to *think* better. This is essential to ensure effectiveness. We can't have peak performance forever. As managerial leaders, we need to focus on the care of our leaders.

Servant leadership focuses us on meeting the needs of our people. But who is ensuring that the leaders are caring for themselves? This is where the leader of leaders must step into the role. It is a form of servant leadership, but it becomes even more important because of the role that managerial leaders play in the success of our organizations. If it is true that there can be no bad organizations and only bad managers, then extra care needs to be taken to ensure the self-care of our leadership.

I often had to be dragged away to eat or sleep by an erstwhile sergeant major during my army career. In command roles in the army, I always had a sergeant major, even as a general. One of the sergeant major roles was to remind me that I was mortal, be brutally honest, and keep an eye on me at all times to ensure that I was taking steps to be resilient. They always knew that if I wasn't getting rest, eating well, and exercising my body, I wouldn't be thinking straight. If I didn't think straight, things could go wrong, with dire effects on people's lives. We need to take this same understanding to our role as managerial leaders.

Leader self-care has both a physical and a mental element to it. But it is the interrelationship of the two, addressing the mental and the physical aspects, that is crucial for managerial leaders to understand on a deep level. If there is a disconnect between the two, then the leader suffers and so do their people. Also, physical wellness improves mental wellness just as mental wellness improves physical wellness. If either is out of sync, the other quickly suffers. It's important to realize that physical fitness enables us to improve our ability to deal with the stressors of day-to-day life. This was clearly the case in Afghanistan when those who were in good physical shape were better able to overcome the wounds they received in battle. While business may not be about improvised explosive devices, it is about the need to be ready and performing every day; therefore, being physically fit is essential for resilience.

PHYSICAL WELLNESS

The principle remains that if you are physically fit and then burn energy to deal with stressors, you are far more resilient and able to get back to stasis than those who are not physically fit. Ensuring that our leaders are physically fit has elements of servant leadership, but it also transcends it. It is necessary for the success of the mission and therefore the strategy. Of course, this now enters the realm of individual rights. So we are not looking to mandate physical fitness but rather to realize that our ability to influence and lead our people will benefit from a certain base level of physical fitness.

Leaders need to realize that in order to influence, they must sell. Selling gets a bad rap these days, as it conjures up tacky used car salesmen and the proverbial snake oil salesmen. Selling is about getting people to want what they need. A good leader *needs* to sell. If we can establish that physical health is something that people need, then it is just a matter of raising their desire to do it. Unlike accountability, it needs to be sold and cannot be mandated. So our leaders must get good at selling and think differently about selling. The first step to that sale, though, is to lead by example to create the inspiration. It cannot be just "Do as I say." We must embody that need and that desire.

MENTAL WELLNESS

It's ironic that most people can see that being in good physical health is something valuable, yet they don't always see mental health in the same way. Mental health is much more of a hidden construct and is not fully understood. There are inroads being made, and many of those come from work in the realm of posttraumatic stress disorder. This is a very important concept that has translated from the military into the civilian world.

Many people think that mental health as an issue in the military began with Afghanistan or Iraq for the United States and Britain. But it actually goes a long way back. While misunderstood as shell shock in the First World War, the signs have always been there. In the military, it became an issue during the 1990s, as Canadians were involved in more and more belligerent peacekeeping operations. The reason that it came to prominence was that the peacekeepers could not control their environment. They had to watch the horrors unfold with no way to control it. It is **Mental wellness came to the forefront during the coronavirus, and we are still unsure of the untold cost the pandemic has had on people's well-being.** important to understand the nature of the need for control as an issue for mental health. As the military began to understand its impact, so, too, did society and business as a whole.

Mental wellness came to the forefront during the coronavirus, and we are still unsure of the untold cost the pandemic has had on people's well-being. At its root was our inability to control. The focus on mental wellness has also required a seismic shift in thinking. We could all understand the physical but did not dare to consider the mental side as well. Mental illness was seen as a failing, in the same way that shell shock was perceived a century before. I use the term *illness* here as the opposite of *wellness*, and there are important reasons that it needs to be seen that way.

Wellness and illness are a spectrum. It is often not thought of this way, as people only perceive mental illness to be at the extreme end. It is also not about institutionalization but rather about the various points on the spectrum moving away from wellness. By working to exercise our body and our mind, we are gaining control. We are making the choices. We are able to get more control of ourselves by engaging in physical fitness. This is why selling it is so important. It is our people's choice and is not a mandated activity. I hated being dragged out of bed at five thirty for a morning run, but now I do it because I know the benefits and I am in control.

SANCTUARY TRAUMA

Looking out for mental wellness then becomes a critical leadership skill. One of the alarming recent mental health statistics runs my blood cold. While it has to do with trauma in the first responder community, it has a bearing on all of us. The statistic was that 50 percent of the trauma that first responders reported was not from an event but from what is known in the field as sanctuary trauma. Sanctuary trauma occurs when an individual who suffered a severe stressor next encounters what was expected to be a supportive and protective environment but discovers only more trauma. It doesn't take much to extrapolate this to the work space. This was a major issue encountering organizations during the pandemic. People faced trauma for their physical safety as they feared infection and physical illness. Then they faced trauma as they worried about employment, financial issues, and concerns for loved ones. The last thing they need is to experience sanctuary trauma in their own work world. Because, after all, many buried themselves in their work to escape the pandemic's difficulties. Being isolated from others added to the trauma, and they sometimes found that their work space exacerbated it. The leaders needed to step in as good servant leaders to protect their people from the organization's pain; otherwise, it made the sanctuary trauma worse.

STABILIZING AND SUSTAINING MENTAL WELLNESS

There are two approaches for leaders to deal with mental wellness. One is to stabilize the employee and the other is to sustain mental wellness. We noticed that our clients were very good at stabilizing and dealing with mental wellness in the work space. By stabilizing, I mean coaching, counseling, offering peer support networks, and scheduling regular sessions to check in with employees. I believe that the stabilizing has done much to reduce the effects of sanctuary trauma. The problem is that it is not necessarily sustainable, so sustainment must take a different tack.

There cannot be a one-and-done solution to sustain mental wellness. Sustaining mental wellness will do much more to reduce sanctuary trauma. It is an ongoing thing. It requires a change to our culture. Mental wellness issues will continue in the years to come—in particular, it is likely the pandemic's legacy. What are the changes needed for our cultures? The first is openness and the ability to discuss mental well-being. It means encouraging people to speak up if they are struggling. This will be the hardest change.

The types of pain that create sanctuary trauma include the following:

* A lack of clarity about what we control

* A lack of clarity of expectations

* Struggles for resources

* Interpersonal challenges

* Unproductive meetings

This pain of sanctuary trauma, while similar to the ideas presented in chapter 2, is about the need for engaged managers and enlightened leaders. In this way, we can sustain mental wellness and reduce sanctuary trauma.

In mental wellness, there is also a contributor known as the *stoic effect*. Again, this was first seen in the military and the first responder community. It is the belief that we just have to suck it up, push through the pain, and show no weakness. This view is hugely detrimental. Our managerial leaders need to be on the lookout for it in their people and particularly in their leaders. Our managerial leaders must be engaged managers and enlightened leaders to bring our organizations to wellness.

It is the bosses who create those engaged managers and enlightened leaders. This is again the skill of the managerial leader of managerial leaders. We need to be vigilant in our thinking. As leaders, it is critical to remember the real influence we have over others. Leaders need to be directed to seek mental wellness and to work to help their people achieve their own mental wellness. In order to help someone else, you must be prepared yourself, such as when, for example, on an airplane they tell you to put your mask on first before helping others. So it is a chain from the managerial leader focusing on their own self-care to leading their leaders in caring for their people. It also requires the manager to look at the system or issues that might cause sanctuary trauma and then get our managers to ensure that the issues don't impact their people. In this way, we are able to both stabilize and sustain mental wellness, which will in turn improve physical wellness. But it all starts with thinking differently about these things.

The Final Overlooked Skill: Follow-Through

Time and time again with clients, I hear the lament that their employees are not doing what they are *supposed* to be doing. The question is always the same: "Did you follow up?" The answer is often, "Well, not really." There are lots of reasons why people don't necessarily complete the tasks that we give them. But the real reason why comes from our own way of thinking. I have found that the skill of following up is a lost art in organizations. It is overlooked in our rush of the tyranny of do. As I mentioned in an earlier chapter, the tyranny of do is about doing and not thinking as we race to move from place to place.

I have been guilty of this far too many times in my career. I ask someone to do something, and I quickly forget about it. It took me a while to realize that I have to ask myself, *If I forgot, why wouldn't they?* I know why I forget. Deep down inside of my thinking, I don't change my approach. Instead of being full of ideas, I need to slow my thinking down, pause, and take my time to detail what the expectations are.

To paraphrase Bill Jensen in his book *Simplicity*, the accountability for the message is with the sender, not the receiver.[8] If we pause and think on that for a moment, it means that the clarity of expectation resides with me, the sender, to be careful to ensure that I am clear about what I am saying and then to make sure that the receiver is clear on what it is that I want. We need to change how we think about the relationship of our messaging. We need to realize that our direct reports are not sitting at our feet waiting for us to spout some insight. They are very much caught up in their own thinking. Twenty years ago when I read Bill's book, it hit me like a lightning bolt! I had assumed people were actively focused on the one thing I was saying, but in reality they are caught up thinking all sorts of *other* things. They considered everything from *How will I do this?* to *I have to remember to get milk on the way home* and everything in between.

---

8   Bill Jensen, *Simplicity.*

TO FOLLOW UP, START AT THE BEGINNING

The starting point for thinking differently about the overlooked skill of follow-through starts at the beginning. It is the nature of our communications and how we send our message. It also includes making sure your listener(s) can clarify back to you what they *thought* they heard. Far too often we miss this step. We don't do it because we are concerned that it looks like we are questioning them and their capability. It is a critical step but one that is too often overlooked, and we need to think differently about our perception of this.

In the army, when we would issue orders to our troops, we would save time at the end to ask the assembled commanders key questions about their role in the plan. This wasn't about catching them unawares but rather to make sure they truly understood our plan and our intent. It's because the leaders are often dead tired, working with very little sleep in very physically demanding circumstances. You need to make sure they are clear on the plan because lives are on the line.

I have often thought this needs to be practiced at work as well. In most cases, we have no idea what people are struggling with on the home front. They might be physically or even emotionally stressed and not on their A game. An ounce of prevention by asking is worth a pound of cure and searching later. This is the first step in follow-through—to make sure everyone is clear on the plan before committing time and resources.

Plan for Follow-Up

There are a multitude of reasons for not following through. But the act of following through needs to be equated with the same importance as the act of telling someone something. It must get the same amount of mind time, so it needs to be planned, and it needs to be negotiated. Our ability as leaders to monitor our people speaks directly to our eventual effectiveness. If we don't monitor, we cannot guarantee success. We can expect them to tell us as they go along, but too often the reality of being human steps in, and people can be reluctant to speak up. They feel that out of their sense of responsibility they have got this, and that can be very dangerous. So we need to plan to monitor and follow up. Follow-through with our leaders on their leadership tasks is one area that falls apart time and time again.

> If we don't monitor, we cannot guarantee success.

Following Up on Leadership Skills

We often naturally follow through on the *task* tasks. Again, it is the nature of our tendency to value task tasks over *people* tasks. Time and again leaders focus on what can easily be measured—the objective and tangible tasks. By their nature, people tasks are subjective and often more intangible. We need to train our thinking in terms of being focused and good at both equally if we are to be effective managerial leaders. When managers of managers and leaders of leaders fail, it is in the follow-up to ensure that the people tasks are being performed to the standard we expect. Our leaders' biggest on the people tasks after not setting clear expectations is the lack of coaching. Again, we assume that fire and forget works, so leaders do not follow up and coach their people. By fire and forget, I mean we issue edicts and then forget to follow up. Instead, we need to be vigilant and on the ball for this at all times.

> **Our leaders' biggest failure on the people tasks after not setting clear expectations is the lack of coaching.**

A few years ago, I sat through a talent assessment exercise with our client. The discussion came up regarding how the individual in question had developed over the year. The manager responded that she was doing an excellent job and that they had been overseeing her success. Interestingly, the manager's peers had a different point of view and felt that there had been no growth in the individual. So the manager of this manager stated that he expected the coaching to continue and that he expected a marked change in the individual's capability over the year. The next year I was there for the individual's assessment, and the situation repeated itself, with the manager claiming once again that the individual had grown further professionally through their coaching, only to be called out by her peers. Later in that year, the manager of the manager confided that the employee had left, and in the exit interview, she cited that she had received no coaching and development whatsoever from her manager. The old adage that employees don't leave companies, only bad bosses, came to mind. Whether it was a case of not valuing the coaching or a lack of skills, the real issue was that waiting a year to find out demonstrably that your managers are coaching or not coaching their people is too long.

Performance Management

Performance management has come under increasing attacks from all corners, and I believe the root of that is the annual aspect of most performance management. If it is only an annual event, it loses credibility and can hardly be seen as development. Part of the annualized nature of performance management is that organizations are too stretched to manage it except on a yearly basis. So it naturally becomes just a box to check off. We need to be mindful that following up *is* performance management.

Coaching for Development

In essence, coaching is what leadership is all about. If you can set your thinking to fixing this one area by being an active manager of your managers in this realm, you will see the growth of your team. Too many clients of ours see development as distinct from work. They view it as a course to be given to someone rather than as development in the work they are doing. This is the real value of coaching. It is about helping performance in the moment and not as some separate event.

Who better to help me perform my work than my boss? That of course means that we as managers of managers need to follow through and ensure that coaching is taking place, especially if our managers do not value it or find themselves caught up in the tyranny of do. It is our way to build future capability and transform the organization. The transformational leader in us needs to step up and lead our leaders to do what should be natural—help them to have conversations about performance. This is our work, and we must set aside time to do it.

> The transformational leader in us needs to step up and lead our leaders to do what should be natural—help them to have conversations about performance.

Stop and Think

Getting your leaders to stop and think about what they need to focus on will help you as well. As managers, we have to set our thinking for how we will follow through to ensure that our managers are doing what they should be doing. We have found that technology is a way to assist managers of managers to follow through, and it also helps the manager to track their own coaching so that they can see the growth and development. We must make it simple for our managers to do, remove the mystique, and enable them to be successful. But it needs a rethink. It must be seen as an integral part of our managers' roles and to be considered as an ongoing thing, not just a once-a-year event. I believe that it starts by thinking about following through first to realize what needs to be done and then working backward from there. Design the system, and make it your own. Start with your ending and plan from what the end state needs to be. It should not be some event tacked on to other things but a separate and distinct plan. This will help you to ultimately achieve your goal of orienting your organization to what is important and transforming it. It all starts with our thinking.

Milestone #7: Skills for You and Your Team

These are skills you will have to revisit frequently at this point on your journey. In your assessment at this stage, you need to be forever vigilant for yourself and your leaders. Wellness is itself a journey, not a destination, so you have the opportunity to make a difference in yours and others' lives every day by focusing on it. Without wellness, you can't handle the difficulties on the journey. In the next chapter, we will discuss the tools available to help you in your role of managing managers.

What is the quality of the thinking in your organization?

How do you know?

What do you need to do differently?

How flexible is your thinking?

How do you know?

What will you do about it?

How well do you challenge the thinking of your team?

How well do your managers challenge the thinking of their teams?

What will you do about it?

How is your physical wellness?

How do you know?

What will you do about it?

How is your mental wellness?

How do you know?

What will you do about it?

How is your managers' physical wellness?

How do you know?

What can you do about it?

How is your managers' mental wellness?

How do you know?

What can you do about it?

Is there potential sanctuary trauma in your organization?

What are the potential causes?

What will you do about it?

How well do you follow up?

How do you know?

What will you do about it?

How well do your leaders follow up?

How do you know?

What will you do about it?

THE TOOLS OF THE MANAGERIAL LEADER

Give me a place to stand and a lever and I will move the world.
—Archimedes

Tools get a bad rap these days. They are seen as superfluous, and the term *tool* is a derisive way to describe someone of very little value. On the other hand, my friend and mentor Jerry Rhodes had another way to describe tools that gets to the very heart of their role in our lives. Jerry described tools as a mechanism to make our work lighter and easier. The analogy he gave was that one can take a screw and use their fingers to twist it into a piece of wood. You can do it, but it requires strength and energy to do so (and a skill to keep it straight as well). A screwdriver helps you do it more effortlessly, thereby improving your efficiency and ultimately your effectiveness (it will go in straighter). Humanity has always developed tools to make our work lighter, from the simplest of levers to the Canadarm on the International Space Station. So tools are integral to efficiency and effectiveness. I believe there are a set of common tools that managerial leaders can employ to make their work easier.

A Cautionary Tale of Tools

There is a cautionary word here on the use of tools: They cannot be replacements for hard work and are not for the slothful managerial leader. They need to add value and assist the individual as an extension of themselves. And here is the other caution: Just as we need to be mindful of the late-night infomercials that sell us things we don't need, we also have to realize there are a plethora of tools that we don't need as well. This is why an effective tool has to be an extension of the manager/leader themselves and not just something that looks shiny and cool. There are lots of tools that were developed by someone at great cost and that are then resold to someone else to defray those costs. We need to be wary of these tools. Technology is replete with examples of this repurposing of things that are not extensions of the work of the managerial leader but that look really cool. Remember, in selling you are getting someone to want something they need, so make sure you need it, too, before you get excited by it.

I believe there are three key tools that the managerial

leaders of managerial leaders can use to improve their world and ease their burden. These are the trilevel team, the after action review, and communications.

The Trilevel Team

The first of these is the trilevel team. As the name suggests, this is a team made up of three levels. The first trilevel team occurs at the director level. The director has a trilevel team made up of their managers and the managers' direct reports: the associates. The second is the first level of the management trilevel, and this is the vice president's trilevel. It includes the directors and the managers. This continues all the way up to the top depending on the nature of the structure, as described earlier. Most organizational structures are based solely on the two-level team or what we call the bilevel team.

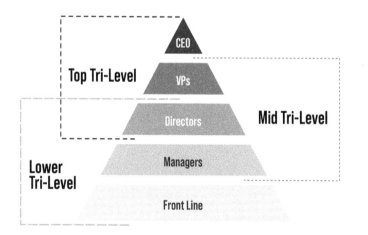

The Role of Trilevel in Alignment

The importance and the value of the trilevel is that it ensures alignment. It is not meant to replace a traditional team, but in our experience, clients who employ the trilevels find that they reduce the silo effect, particularly when the first trilevel is at the executive level. It is through the trilevel that teams achieve lateral integration. The trilevel has a unique way to enhance trust because it builds trust and understanding at all three levels by showing that there is oversight on the bilevel to ensure that it is integrated to other teams. It also reinforces trust in management because, by its nature, it focuses on the leadership and can ensure that no management team is on a breakaway. This is particularly true because it cascades down from the CEO throughout the organization.

No More Broken Telephones

In the typical five-level organization, there are only three trilevels. The importance of this is that it helps to break the proverbial broken telephone character of the binary nature of the manager-direct report relationship. The broken telephone is overcome because any cascading messaging is taken in twice before a manager passes it to their direct reports. In this way, it is an important tool to cascade messaging, including strategy and objectives.

As mentioned earlier, learning in a trilevel is a key tool for developing leaders by having them attend training with their manager and manager once removed, because it drives home the accountability to think and then behave differently. It again reinforces trust in the leadership when they can hear from their manager once removed with enough context to add value to their work.

Several of our clients use it as a way to fulfill the accountability of the manager once removed to develop the talent pool. The trilevel meeting enables the manager once removed to see their direct reports once removed in a setting to better assess the talent farther down for succession plans. They are able to see the members of the talent pool and better assess the types of development they require.

Trilevel Applications

The trilevel meeting is a useful tool to define process two levels down. Often the managers in the middle don't understand the nature of the process, and the manager once removed is expecting things to work well. The problem is that there is no way to get this clarity in the other formats for meetings, such as the bilevel. Our clients also use it as the means to define authority laterally as they work to resolve role clarity and keep the business out of silos and working laterally.

In the case of a major utility company we were working with, there were over seventy people in the CEO's trilevel. Where one might first think it involved a lot of sitting around, it was facilitated in such a way as to keep it moving while being focused on resolving issues that were creating tension and friction. Those in attendance for the first trilevel were engaged throughout in discussion of issues and found it invaluable to understand who did what and how the work needed to flow across the business.

Often the feedback we get when proposing the system is that too many people are involved. You have to use judgment and discretion, and the largest trilevels are at the director-manager-associate level. This can get into the thousands, so it has to be done judiciously. In the case of a manufacturing client, where there are literally thousands of associates, there are always supervisory roles, and they become part of the trilevel. This does not necessarily include all of the employees. Depending on the nature of the meeting, this may be all that you need. It ensures that the supervisors are on the same page as the managers and directors and enhances a common operating picture of management.

The largest trilevel I have facilitated was just under one hundred employees in manufacturing at the director to supervisor level. The important thing to remember in planning these is to be clear on what you are trying to achieve. This will define the makeup of the meeting. In the case of my manufacturing example, it was to implement a new system, so it needed input and engagement of the supervisors, but it also had to ensure that the managers were aware of the system. This also speaks to the other value of the trilevel in that it becomes a great tool to socialize changes that are coming into an organization. As with all things, it requires significant planning.

In regard to frequency, before the pandemic, many CEOs had a cadence of quarterly trilevels. However, the nature of distributed workforces made it almost untenable because one could not engage in a dialogue, and so the trilevels instead became ways to pass information. As those companies return to the office, it will be interesting to see how many go right back to their trilevel cadence postpandemic.

The trilevel becomes a tool to extend the reach of the manager once removed. It is a tool to assist in providing clarity and trust both for and within management. Most importantly, it acts as the mechanism to get lateral integration and context to the various levels of management.

The After Action Review

The after action review is a thinking tool as well as a transformation tool, and it was also adapted from the military. Started by the US Army in the 1970s to improve the training and development of soldiers, it gradually morphed into business in the 1990s. The essence of the after action review (AAR) is a process to study a situation or circumstance to determine what happened, why it happened, and how to improve or sustain performance. In the military, it is used during training events to stop the exercises and review what happened, enabling the participants to learn in the moment and either adjust or reinforce behaviors. What makes it unique from coaching or feedback is the approach. During the AAR, the participants learn as a group through reflection. The AARs are facilitated events by an unbiased individual whose role is to ask questions to help participants explore what happened and why. In this way, the onus is on the individual to reflect on and express their learning.

In big military exercises, I have seen huge groups of troops grind to a halt to conduct an AAR and then reset and start at it again based on what they have learned. It is quite a sight to see an all-out simulated attack come to an abrupt stop and watch the flipchart brought out as the group gathers in a semicircle to discuss what has transpired. The lowest private to the officers walk away with lessons learned, and with that knowledge, they can then put that learning immediately back into practice. Key to the process is for the individual to reflect and then identify the action to take to reinforce or improve. For this to work, it is essential for it to be facilitated by an impartial third party whose only concern is to help others learn.

> **Key to the process is for the individual to reflect and then identify the action to take to reinforce or improve.**

These principles were carried into the field of battle during the Afghan war by Canadian troops, and while they didn't stop the fight to learn, they very quickly conducted the AAR once out of the operation. In this way, lessons learned from the field were fed back to Canada to improve training at home before the next contingents headed into operations. The AAR, after all, is really the manifestation of continuous improvement.

We encourage our clients to utilize the process to help resolve issues and create learning organizations. An important premise is that there is never one cause to an issue, and long-standing systemic problems can be removed by building in time to reflect on and review how things happened.

Recently we assisted a North American utility by using the process to resolve a big customer service issue. In the middle of winter, customers had no power as a result of a shortage of spare parts. Each department had a view as to whose fault it was, ranging from customer service to technical service to supply chain, and everyone was blaming each other. We facilitated a meeting of the key leadership to review what should have happened versus what did happen and then explored what could have been done to mitigate the issue. In the end there were over twenty actions identified that could be done to improve the situation, and the departments were able to swiftly implement them without wasting time pointing fingers. Too many times, in my experience, we are prone to blame others and find that one thing that is at fault. In reality it is never the one thing, and the only way to resolve it is to reflect and think it through.

APPLICATION OF THE AAR

The AAR in the NATO armies is a very structured approach and is developed to meet specific training requirements.

> It reduces perfectionism by clarifying that we all make mistakes and that mistakes are not fatal if we learn from them.

We have proven that the principles can be applied to business in a way that meets the just-enough requirement. But its application can have secondary benefits as well. It naturally opens up people to learn on the job by demonstrating learning opportunities. It reduces perfectionism by clarifying that we all make mistakes and that mistakes are not fatal if we learn from them. It solves technical issues while raising confidence and trust in the organization, ultimately creating actionable change that improves the organization.

THE MANAGER OF MANAGERS AND THE AAR

The manager of managers has a critical role to play in being the sponsor of AAR activities. The AAR is a process, but it is also a mindset, and the mindset is a healthy addition to any organization. I often ask organizations if they are, or want to be, learning organizations. Invariably people say yes, but it comes with the warning that you have to be of the mentality that you can accept mistakes. Too often unattainable perfectionism gets in our way, and we expect perfection from others. The AAR builds the belief that we can accept mistakes and that we learn from them. As Churchill said, "Failure isn't fatal and success isn't forever." The mindset makes it different from the postmortem. It is not about explaining why something happened so much as what we learned from it for next time. The leader of leaders needs to sponsor it and see that it is not just a one-off event. They ensure that it becomes a way of being and sustain its use. It needs to be sanctioned and encouraged by the boss. Organizations that have fully embraced the AAR have seen engagement go up demonstrably.

At Forrest & Company, we have an AAR after every training session, sometimes no more than fifteen minutes long. In other cases, when an issue arises with a client, it is worth spending more time. And by the way, often a lot of the issues are created by me, so it is important for me to embrace it so that we (I) don't do it again. The leader of leaders can facilitate the meetings, and while not always ideal, it often is the only way. The leader of leaders then has to conduct it in such a way as to be neutral and not steer it, especially when they may be implicated. This becomes easier with practice, and a good dose of humility builds trust.

The AAR is a simple yet profoundly transformational tool. It can change culture, but as with so many of the elements of managerial leadership, it requires discipline and consistency. All it takes, though, is for one leader of leaders to implement it, and it starts to gain traction to begin the transformation. And who can argue with learning from mistakes?

Communication as a Tool

The essential managerial leadership tool is communication. Good communication eases work and reduces rework. It leads to efficiency, effectiveness, and adaptability. But ultimately it builds trust. In recent years I have gradually come to realize just how important communication is. I decried communication training in the past, but I have now

> Good communication eases work and reduces rework.

come around to its importance. As I have said, only through communication can two brains work together. So this tool used well really does make your life easier. The professional managerial leader needs to embrace this as *their* tool. It is something that can be learned but requires practice and use, as otherwise it gets rusty. The professional managerial leader makes this an ongoing learning goal.

We learn to communicate from birth, but very few of us in managerial leadership roles work to become a professional at it. So our communication patterns get set at early ages. As managerial leaders, we need to fully comprehend that clarity of communication is key to helping us and helping our people. The servant leader understands this and ensures their people understand intent and are clear on expectations.

As you have seen throughout the book, communication comes up time and again. It is a broad topic, and I won't go into great lengths describing it except to mention that it is indeed a tool, how you can best make use of it, and where I have seen issues with it. As a tool, it is constituted with written and verbal communication. As a tool, it can be very powerful in these two instances, but when it is not handled well, it can instantly damage trust and wreak havoc. We have all seen examples of the not-well-thought-out email that inadvertently raises hackles and upsets equilibrium.

EMAIL AS COMMUNICATION

Time and again when working with teams, the issue of email communications comes up. In my army life, we had a staff school that taught officers how to write. Of course, school and university taught a way of written communication, but at staff school, we learned a specific method, and eventually I also taught how to write the military way.

Everything was standardized, and one knew exact spacing, indentation, numbering, and date assignment, but more importantly we learned how to get the message across. In those days, you drafted your correspondence, sent it to the clerk to format it, and then it was mailed out. I remember well when we introduced email into the military. The old sweats, myself included, decried it. The standards would drop, and there would be an avalanche of communications.

Today, looking back, I am sorry I wasn't wrong. This is exactly what has happened in the military and in business. The military took up email and then they closed the staff school. From then on, standardization was abandoned, and in a lot of cases, it fell to individual commanders to establish the standards they expected for communication. This is now the case in business as well. But too often leaders are unwilling to clarify their expectations. This leads to guesswork at best and often confusion and disarray.

There is no standard for business communication. The military still has its manuals and the subject continues to be taught, but I have yet to find any consistency in business. Sure, those with MBAs learn, and there are style books but not necessarily about what needs to be expressed. Educational institutions have an approach to communication that builds from narrative to conclusion. Military writing works the other way. It starts with what the receiver needs to know first and then follows with the supporting information. The premise is

THE MANAGERIAL LEADERSHIP JOURNEY

simple: in battle, when flooded with information, you must get to the point quickly. The US military has a name for this: bottom line up front (BLUF). BLUF has made it into the lexicon of allied armies and is rooted in the same teaching I did at the staff school. However, I have found that this principle is not used extensively in business. In my executive coaching, I make it a point to raise both for my coaching clients, and I suggest they pass this to their teams. There are far too many emails out there, and too often they meander and are unclear. BLUF is a good way to counter this, but people will not get there on their own. They will need to be led, and so it is important for leaders of leaders to hone this tool.

THE EMAIL EPIDEMIC

In a similar vein, the issue of email proliferation is an epidemic in business. Clients who routinely tell me of thousands of unread emails is a symptom. They say this means that those emails are obviously not that important to the sender. I am guilty of poor email etiquette at times myself. Mobile phones have made it worse because it allows us to triage and never really escape the mail. The pandemic heightened this when everyone felt the need to stay in touch. The epidemic is exacerbated when we introduce different technologies, and soon you never know where to look for the messages. Slack and Zoom are only a few examples of the proliferation.

In my experience, the organizations that are truly on the path to stopping the email epidemic are those where the CEO has taken an active interest and set the standard for the organization. Taking the time to do this and establishing expectations is critical. Email is a tool, but it is one that is used haphazardly. Just as there is danger when using a power tool without safety goggles, email can come back to hurt you. The best examples of standards are clear subject headings, BLUF selective distribution lists, and cutting out cc emails. As one CEO stated, if you cc someone, do not expect them to read it, so therefore don't send it. Too often cc is just CYA. When leaders begin speaking out against cc'ing, it stops being about covering your ass and becomes about building trust.

At the same time, as the proliferation of email and chat functions occurred, there was a commensurate drop in people picking up the phone to discuss issues. The result is that communications become unclear. Voice-to-voice communication is still the better method to ensure clarity because it becomes a dialogue, as I discussed earlier. If you accept my premise that communications is a tool for the manager of managers, then it is up to them to see that it is used well to ensure that people get what they need to do their jobs.

Battle Rhythm

The most powerful way communication becomes a tool is in the creation of battle rhythm. Battle rhythm is about planning. Planning starts at the top. Battle rhythm

Battle rhythm is about how you pass direction down to the levels below to allow them to react, plan, and direct action as quickly as possible.

is about how you pass direction down to the levels below to allow them to react, plan, and direct action as quickly as possible. Battle rhythm is where planning and communication come together, and it links the two. Specifically, it is where you bring your team together to get their input into your decisions. Then you decide, and the clock starts. They then have their meeting with their teams to get their input and then make their decisions and issue their direction. Then the next level does the same, all the way down, so that the front line can get to action as quickly as possible. Given that it must be touched during the cascade all the way down by each level of management, you need to build in time for this to happen. This way, those on the front line aren't running to catch up or going in half-cocked. Good structure enables this. To do the planning requires forethought of what might happen, insight of what is happening, and hindsight of what happened.

Too often I see that we as managerial leaders lose sight of where we are in the organization. I use a tool to ask, "How many employees report up to you?" The immediate answer is the team of direct reports because we are caught in the paradigm of our team. We need to be mindful of all the dozens, hundreds, or thousands who are below, waiting on our direction. It is because of this that battle rhythm is so important.

BATTLE RHYTHM DEFINED

The concept of battle rhythm comes from the military, but it is a necessity of managerial hierarchies. We give it the name to maintain an orderly routine with constancy and consistency for communication. It enables you to synchronize activities, and this is particularly important in hierarchies. Too often CEOs say, "Let's go this way" and expect that the ship is turning. The problem is that the thousands of human beings are going about their business and need to be steered. Remembering what has to happen farther down is senior leaders' important awareness. This worsens if senior leadership takes too much time planning or dawdles over decisions, which leaves everyone farther down scrambling to make the deadline. Synchronization becomes really important in multinational corporations or those covering multiple time zones. Good battle rhythm enables you to deal with crises yet keep things moving along. It is really important in the military, especially when people are tired and stressed, and I believe it is exactly the same for business. This is where the constancy comes in handy.

BATTLE RHYTHM AS CONTROL

Battle rhythm is about control. I hear continually from all levels of our clients how many meetings they are in now and how many of those meetings don't add value. Time is being wasted, and people's efforts are being wasted. People forget that when you ask someone to attend your meeting, you are asking them to stop doing their work and start doing yours. Battle rhythm controls the meetings to organize and direct the energies of the organization. In the age of a distributed workforce, we have people trying desperately to stay in touch and people feeling guilty that they are working from home. This needs to be balanced to get things done and enable people to react and think.

BATTLE RHYTHM AS STRUCTURE

Battle rhythm is about structure. How long should it take from you deciding what needs to be done to when it is actioned at the front line? Battle rhythm streamlines this so that you can adapt more quickly. Poor structure means that it will take longer. Your organization needs a good rhythm, and cadence will enable everyone to do their job. Good battle rhythm allows you to adapt. It is about going from idea to implementation quickly.

Battle rhythm is also about planning when people need to be together and synchronize from the top down. It is best designed based on the strategy and the value chain of the business. Clarity of the organizational structure enables it to work effectively, and understanding of accountabilities and authorities further supercharges battle rhythm. It requires discipline to stick to it, but in the end, it will enable better decision-making and improve your efficiency. It does require looking at the whole enterprise from top to bottom to enable strategic, operational, and tactical activities. A guiding principle is to keep as much space as needed in your battle rhythm to give you flexibility. I have found that busi-

> Your organization needs a good rhythm, and cadence will enable everyone to do their job.

nesses that use project management constructs are able to further enhance their battle rhythm. Finally, the battle rhythm should also include the standards and expectations for communications, including meetings. The tactical aspects of meetings seem to have been lost on business lately. These include who should be in attendance, clarity of intent, and agendas and time management.

Battle rhythm is the work of managers of managers. It is designed to enable the execution to occur at the lowest levels, and it is an important tool in the tool belt of the manager of managers. With it you can connect the leadership to their tasks while giving them the time to fulfill their roles without overwhelming them. Not paying attention to the organization's rhythm leads it to vagaries, and the professional managerial leader should reduce caprice wherever possible to keep the organization in fighting trim.

These are just three tools that managers of managers can use to lead their people. There are others, but you can launch your leaders and create a professional managerial leadership culture with these three. The trilevel

> Professional communication approaches are the glue that binds your leadership together.

enables you to align your management teams. The AAR helps to build a culture of professional development. Professional communication approaches are the glue that binds your leadership together.

Milestone #8: The Tools of Management

As you contemplate this final milestone in your journey, the tools here may or may not move the world, but their disciplined use will help you and your leaders immeasurably. Before you can use these tools, you need that place to stand. Each of the previous points on the journey have led you to this point. They have given you your place to stand.

How laterally integrated are your teams?

How do you know?

What do you need to do differently?

How can you use trilevel team meetings?

How can your direct reports?

What is your rhythm for their use?

How good are you at assessing why things go wrong?

How good are you at assessing why things go right?

What are examples of where you could have used an AAR to find out what happened?

Is your organization a learning organization?

How do you know?

How can you use the AAR to learn better?

What needs to change in emails?

What needs to change in meetings?

What will you do differently?

How good is your organizational cadence?

How do you know?

What will you do about it?

How could you improve your battle rhythm?

Could your managers improve their battle rhythm?

What will you do about it?

Do your people live by the values?

Do your managers drive home the values?

What will you do about it?

How effective is your knowledge management?

Do your people share information well?

What are the opportunities to improve knowledge sharing?

CONCLUSION

The journey of self-understanding is never done.

That leadership journey that began when I was nineteen years old was my basic officer training. We had a grizzled old captain who was our course officer. He wasn't what you see in the movies. Instead, he had a clear image of what he was trying to build. Unlike the Hollywood representation of the five thirty morning run, we sang "You Are My Sunshine," and he treated everyone with respect. He imparted to me that an officer must be first and foremost an officer and a gentleman simultaneously. That is not a trite phrase. He had seen all sorts in his career, and he wanted us to be clear that there was a sacred covenant with the leader and the led. His message has resounded with me throughout all these years: that it requires discipline and that your work as a leader never ends. At the end of the course, he gave a speech in which he made it clear that we were all on a lifelong journey, and we would need to be disciplined to learn every day in our careers.

My journey continues in my day-to-day work with clients, and while I have a very small team now in place of the thousands before, I am still learning every day.

Your journey is not done. It is one that you can carry on throughout your career and life, whether at home with family or in those outside interests that energize you to face the challenges of your work life. This was not meant to be a book about the sole steps of the journey but merely the key ones to consider along the way. Recognize that all human endeavor is governed by managerial leadership and that we need to hone those abilities. Creating that professional outlook enables you to force multiply your success by honing skills of managing managers. Those managers need to understand that accountability separates the professional from the amateur. Because in today's world, we need engaged employees to use their judgment and discretion, and it starts first with engaged managers who know themselves and where they are going so that they can stand tall in the face of the storms around them. Knowing where they are going is the ability to plan and to adapt the plan as the circumstances change. If you have taken the time to heed them, they will have furnished you with an insight and understanding to develop other skills and build new tools.

The journey need not be alone. There are other tools and tricks available to you at our website. Begin to take that unconventional business pursuit—the managerial leadership journey. My goal has been not only to give you information but also to challenge your thinking to be the most enlightened leader and engaged manager possible.

Everything written here has been to show that you are part of the proud profession of management, without which there can be no organizational or societal successes. This is the essence of the managerial leader. All human endeavor needs leadership and management in order to be the best that we can be.

A Call to Action

Armed with the information here, it's time to embark on the final part of your journey. Take all that is here and use it, whether in for-profit or nonprofit organizations, to create the new world where human beings are valued and raised to be the best that they can be to lead our planet going forward. While on your journey, if you need companionship, a battle buddy, or help, please feel free to reach out to me at:

ManagerialLeadershipJourney.com.